Safe at Home

"Why don't you just tell him you're not going to Florida?" my mother says.

"You know I can't do that. He's my husband. I have to go where he goes."

"Well, at least Charles doesn't gamble. I scrimp and save and Phil throws his whole week's salary away at the craps table at the Bachelor's Club."

"Don't let him go there," my aunt says.

"What can I do? I can't stop him."

I go upstairs to change into my play clothes, wondering about these two women: Do they think if God hears them say something good about their lives, He'll sweep down, take the good thing away, and put a curse on them?

About a year later they'd switched from drinking coffee to whiskey, and when I'd come home Aunt Adele would tell me to very quiet, that my mother wasn't feeling well, that she was taking a nap.

How many millennia has this been going on between lonely, desperate women? There's that to think about.

But there's also this: they sickened me, these little betrayals of relationships and marriages, and frightened me—how easily the two women passed judgments, the way you'd ask someone to pass the salt or pepper over a nicely seasoned meal, then sprinkle too much of one or the other and complain about *that*.

Could be that's when I decided the only safe course of action would be to keep my head down and to be as perfect as possible. At everything.

Crazy in the Family

JACK'S SISTER SUFFERED FROM SCHIZOPHRENIA. One day as a kid, about thirteen-years-old, he came home from school to see men taking Roberta away in a straitjacket.

A brief history of the dawn of pharmaceutical therapy: medications for mental illness weren't available until after World War II. Officers suffering from mental illness saw psychiatrists, but they rarely improved. Enlisted men were given Thorazine and did get better, the first indication that some mental illnesses had a physical basis—not problems caused by bad mothers.

My family had misgivings about Jack that ranged from his sister's, Aunt Sarah's, assessment—(*He's a bum. He gambles. He runs after women.*) to my parents'—(*He's got crazy in his family.*) meaning, Roberta. I was enraged, at eighteen, that they thought that way. Jack and I would drive to Ligonier—a very expensive private hospital his father had insisted upon—to visit Roberta. You had to call ahead to make arrangements, to give the attendants time to clean her up. When she was violent she was strapped down, splayed to the bed with three-inch leather straps on her wrists and ankles. Eventually, the lobotomy was ordered.

You can understand why I never gave up on my daughter Lauren. When *she* was eighteen and went crazy...there is no greater pain.

Insanity will always be in our lives, but I couldn't bear the thought of her dead—ever—even after the first suicide attempt.

Yes, she wanted to die. *I* wanted to die, too.

We Need to Talk About Lauren

THE FIRST SIGNS APPEARED IN kindergarten. I'd prompt her with nursery rhymes: *Jack and Jill went up the hill to fetch a pail of...* She said nothing. The teacher administered a test to all the children—at the same time—to determine their readiness for first grade. Lauren marked the first box as the answer to every question. Maybe my daughter would do better, I suggested, if you could...

"I don't have time to give each child the test individually," the teacher said. She was furious. This was the woman who had tied Lauren to a chair and put tape over her mouth because she talked too much.

So, go figure, I took my daughter to a psychiatrist when she was five.

"Don't worry, Mother," he said. "She's perfectly fine. Just relax. She does bite her nails, though."

First of all, I wasn't his mother, and secondly, I was relaxed. This was my third child. And she didn't bite her nails.

Lauren was so terrified by first grade that she'd lift up her desk top and vomit into the maw of its metal cavity.

I called the fancy private school that my older daughter attended; Lauren was accepted right away. "Don't you want to test her or anything?" I asked.

"Any member of your family is welcome here."

After a second year in first grade, the school called to say Lauren had to leave. They couldn't handle her.

So, back to public school where Lauren was put in special ed. The stigma was so bad that her brother Richard cried, pleaded with me, "Please don't. I'll tutor her every day."

Kids Lauren's age had already started calling her "Retard"—and Lauren's friend, who had wine-stain birthmarks, "Spots."

But the special ed teacher, Mrs. Rosenthal, was wonderful; Lauren thrived. At the end of the year, though, the school told me her I.Q. was too high—she'd have to go back to regular first grade, even though she'd be two years older than the rest of the kids.

I was desperate. I appealed to Catholic schools, to a different private school. Finally Jack found out about a new private school that made a place for Lauren. One day she could explain condensation and evaporation like a miniature scientist. The next day she couldn't add two and two. Yet, there, ten years later, she graduated with her senior class.

Then came the community college and her first schizophrenic breakdown.

Retarded Day

I HAD COME A LONG way to become the teacher I wanted to be: Pennsylvania to Utah, with a span of ten years in between the two points.

Now I taught reading to special-education children in grades kindergarten through fifth grade. Mildly retarded, behaviorally disturbed, dyslexic, physically disabled—twenty-two of them, far too many given the range of ages and difficulties. But with enough time and patience, I could coax a little boy, for example, with an I.Q. of forty-eight to read twenty-two books (albeit, easy books) in a year.

Some days we had opera day. My aide Loretta would sing, "Pleeease come to your reading group nowww." The children would have to sing permission to go to the restroom. There was gym day: you had to do a somersault or some other feat and point to the hall pass.

One morning, one of my students noticed the janitor, George, cleaning the paned windows of our classroom door. "He's retarded, you know," she said. That was the moment I realized none of the kids knew they had special needs.

I don't remember whose idea it was, mine or Loretta's, but a day for special-needs children was officially designated. We'd be fired for it now—but on that day everyone at the school had to arrive with a handicap. Some were blindfolded or wore earplugs; some were on crutches or in a wheel chair. By noon some had had it with their afflictions, but I told them, *No. You have one day, all day, at this. Now you know what it's like for children who struggle all their lives.*

Probably rumors spread about how much fun those "retarded" kids and I had. One day a small boy approached me on the playground. "I keep not paying attention in my class every day, and they still won't put me in yours."

Break

THE NIGHT AFTER CHRISTMAS, LAUREN crawled into my king-sized bed with me, something she hadn't done since she was a little girl with nightmares. I was getting used to the roominess of the bed without Jack in it, but moving our furniture and belongings into this small apartment had been like stuffing a size nine foot into a size six shoe.

A week before the holiday Lauren had knocked on each door in the building, apologizing in advance for making too much noise. I was busy baking Banbury tarts, pretending to still be a family, to give much notice to her behavior. Lauren often did strange things, which was why she'd been seeing a psychiatrist for the past two years, Dr. Charney, who I would eventually learn had extremely unethical, not to mention illegal, methods of treating a vulnerable teenager.

Two o'clock in the morning. I popped out of slumber like a diver with an empty tank surfacing for air. Lauren was sitting straight up, eyes wide open and glazed.

"What time is it? Tell me, what time is it? I'm going to die at seven. Feel my heart," she said, grabbing my hand, pressing it to her chest.

"Eighteen-year-olds don't die of heart attacks," I said. "You've just had a bad dream. Nothing's going to happen to you." I closed my eyes and felt her lie down beside me for a moment.

"I'm in my coffin. Right, Mother? I'm in my coffin." Her eyes were febrile lights. She was screaming now, "And you're dead. You're dead, too, aren't you, Mother?"

"No, no, of course I'm not dead!" I put my arms around her, feeling the heat of her body through her nightshirt. "Please, baby, don't. You've just had a nightmare. Try to calm down. You'll wake all the neighbors."

Then she was up, moving in a frenzy around the room. Her words came fast. "I'm black. Nobody knew it, but I did. I was born black." Her long dark hair fell in wisps around her face. "Remember how you got me mixed up with the black baby when I was born? The nurses took me to the black couple because I was so dark. I really am black. You lied." She dipped her fingers in her ashtray and smeared cigarette ashes over her face.

"You're not black!"

"I'm an Indian!" she shouted, pantomiming a war dance around a campfire, patting her hand against her mouth, whooping. "I've always been an Indian. A black Indian. That's why everyone hates me."

"No one hates you! Come back to bed!"

"The fire, the fire! They burned my eyes out. I'm blind, Mother. I can't see. I'm blind!"

I pulled her away from the blaze that only she saw.

At four a.m. I dialed the psychiatrist.

"Just go back to sleep, Mother," he said.

Mother?

"She couldn't have a break all at once like that. I just saw her two days ago, on Thursday. It's impossible to get sick that fast." He hung up, and I stood listening to nothing but the sound of a receiver off the hook: *beepbeepbeep.*

For three hours Lauren and I struggled together in the master bedroom, trapped in a night that seemed unable to move toward sunrise.

"Jesus! I'm the first woman Jesus dying for the sins of mankind! I'm going to die on the cross. Kyrie eleison, kyrie, kyrie! Lord have mercy! Fire. Fire! I'm not going. I don't want to go. My tears, look at them, Mother, they've turned to blood. And flies, millions of flies are crawling out of the corners of my eyes and swarming away!"

I tried to hold her in my arms. "You're all right. You're safe. I'm here." She pulled away.

"I AM going to die at seven," she sobbed. "Don't leave me. Help me, Mother, help me!"

The second hand crept around the dial. One minute after seven. Another and another. We held onto each other on the bed like two people shipwrecked, afloat on a life raft. The cold light of morning seeped in behind the blinds. Lauren was shivering violently. I wrapped her in blankets in our big brown chair and called the doctor again.

"Drive her to my office and I'll have a look at her if you insist," he said with weary resignation.

In the back of the elevator was a shriveled, old man wearing a soiled overcoat sizes too large for him.

"Hi, how are you?" Lauren said, wrapping herself around him, kissing his face.

"What? I should know you?" he muttered, pushing away. "*Meshuga.*"

In the waiting room, Lauren danced like a live wire on the pavement, downed in a wind storm. She perched on the edge of the leather sofa, jumped up again, rifled through old magazines, paced, babbled to the receptionist and to another client, trying to hide behind his newspaper. She pulled her sweater over her head, unzipped her jeans and began shoving them below her hips.

"No!" I said.

Her mouth shaped itself into an O, the startled look I'd once seen on her face as a baby.

The wipers swept away the dusting of snow on the windshield. *Clickswish, clickswish.* Lauren: talkingtalkingtalking all the way to St. Francis Hospital, a dreary building, dark with soot.

"Lauren, you're going to stay here for a while. The doctors will help you feel better."

My daughter, beside me at the admissions desk, spoke into an imaginary phone. "Hello, yes, sure, I see. No. No. I won't do that. You shouldn't *say* that. Mother, he called me a dirty Jew!"

"Who?"

"He did. Dad on the phone."

"He's not on the phone."

"Oh, yes he is. On the television. You don't understand. He said, 'You're a dirty Jew.'" Her lips stretched across her teeth into a grotesque grin. She laughed, laughedlaughedlaughed.

A nurse rode with us in the elevator to the psychiatric ward. The door slid open and a second door, glass, reinforced with steel mesh, blocked our way. She pushed the HOLD button, selected a key from a ring of keys big as a plate, opening then locking the second door behind us.

The ward: sagging Naugahyde sofas, thread-worn chairs, a TV, the nurses' station. Voices on the P.A., squawking.

"How are we today?" a new nurse asked.

Lauren giggled.

Women, old, young, thin, fat, stared with lost, empty eyes at the TV. An overheated smell: disinfectant and stale cigarette smoke. A frail old lady swaying back and forth, clinging to a barred window saying, "Mother, mother, mother." An obese girl, sitting on the yellowing linoleum under the fluorescent lights, engaged in angry conversation alone. Two burly men in white shirts and pants, leaned against the wall, smoking.

We were led to a small room with a narrow hospital bed. The window overlooked a cemetery. The nurse recited a litany of rules: no matches, no belts, no sharp instruments, nothing made of glass.

Lauren laughed. "I had a dream, Mother. Birds were flying out of my vagina. Isn't that funny?"

"Time to say good-bye," the nurse said.

"I want to go with you, Mother," Lauren said.

"You have to stay. But I'll be back tomorrow," I said.

At the elevator, Lauren tried to get on, extending one leg for a giant step forward like a cartoon character. The nurse restrained her.

"I'm going with you!" Lauren lunged.

"You'll just be here for a little while," I said, "until you feel better."

"You can't leave me here!" Lauren shoved the nurse. "Mother, don't leave me!"

And then the orderlies had her pinned by the arms and the elevator door slid shut.

In the hospital lobby, then through the doors into a cold, wintry day, I thought I could still hear her screams.

And I left her there, I had to, that one time. Not only couldn't I reach her mind, now I couldn't reach her, her flesh.

I had been left behind myself with Mutah, my grandmother, when I was two weeks old then reclaimed when I was three. So, somewhere inside of me, I knew the pain of that: abandonment.

I swore: never again.

The drive to the hospital each day was like crossing the desert on my knees. Repentance. I took Lauren gifts of atonement: watercolors and paper, cigarettes, soap. The day I brought a sack of bright red apples, she took one, held it at arm's length and tried to take a bite of air. I bent her elbow and guided the apple to her lips.

Her joints grew stiff from the Haldol. She drooled. Her hands shook. We tried to sit together in the common room. She'd dash down the hall, doing cartwheels in the narrow corridor.

I'm here if you want to be with me. I chase you, but you can't keep running. I saw that sly look on your face when you covered it with cigarette ash. You wanted to shock me. You want my undivided attention. You yell, "I'm still here, Mother!" It's a sort of game, isn't it? What do you want me to do? I pretend I'm reading the book I brought with me. Now what? You won't open your eyes, won't look at me. You tell me you're a clown, spreading the ashes on your face. I tell you that clowns use white makeup, and you apply deodorant and liquid soap.

"Would you like to see Tommy?" I asked.

"Oh, he's already here."

Only when it was time for me to leave did Lauren come out of her fog of hallucinations and delusions to protest being left behind.

Every day I rode down in the elevator and walked past the cemetery to my car, staring at the snow-blanketed graves, wishing I could lie down atop one and be absorbed into the earth.

The Least I Could Do

WE DID HAVE TO BORROW money—quite a lot of it—from Tommy's brother, a physician. So that explains the van and sneaking into motel swimming pools. We were frugal; we had to be.

In a strange way, though, I loved our circumstances. I loved sitting in the comfy captain's chair while Tommy drove, listening to the radio, eating granola and dried fruits and nuts, the two of us talking and talking. I'd put my bare feet up on the dashboard and watch the endless broken white line on the road go by mile after mile.

I thought of my life as being in two parts: a (sham) conventional life in Pittsburgh with a (cheating) husband, three children, a springer spaniel, a nice house, a country-club membership, and now this one, adventurous, with a sexy (much) younger man who had this crazy idea he was going to make it as a baseball agent. At least the life Tommy and I lived in the van was real. But weeks went by on the road without a single player signed—and I'd get scared. What was I doing? I should be with a man about to retire, not one just starting out on a pipe-dream of a career.

Then again, if you look up *ne'er-do-well* in the dictionary you'll see a picture of Jack with me standing right next to him. I don't remember the exact order now, but he started and gave up on one business after another. First came the cigarette-vending machines. A pack of cigarettes cost twenty-two cents then; the vending machine accepted only quarters. We had to buy a little gizmo that slit the cellophane off the pack, and then I'd stuff three cents change into each one. He and his buddy Herbie sold that enterprise to the Mafia.

There was the record business. He and Herbie had one client with a hit record, then—kaput. He sold freezers to apartment dwellers. He upholstered car seats. He opened a nightclub for upper-class blacks; Aretha Franklin headlined there once. He owned a bar.

Whatever Jack went into I was by his side. My father was a gambling addict, so you could say I was natural for the job of being Jack's wife. I was his bookkeeper and his assistant, an amorphous title that had me doing whatever he needed me to do. When Jack built a bowling alley with his cousin in Baden, Pennsylvania, for example, they needed someone who was a certified bowling instructor, which meant taking a test. I was good at tests, so, no surprise, I passed, got a badge to sew on my sleeve, and received a certificate along with my own bowling ball and orange bowling shoes. The trouble was my best score on the lanes, ever, was thirty-four. Once as a joke I took a dentistry test and scored a hundred percent.

In between failures—Jack took pride in the fact that he could tell when something wasn't going to make it and knew when to "get out in time"—my husband would go back to his family's auto-parts business, which he hated.

The least I could do was give Tommy a chance. Neither of us had a clue what it would take to be a baseball agent. He was persevering, but sometimes he did lose faith and want to quit.

I'd yell at him. "You want to be like Jack? Start something and then give up? I'm tired of being with quitters! How will you pay your brother back?"

I feel badly about the yelling now. But when we finally made it, got that first player to sign a contract, Tommy said he couldn't have done it without me. That was the best moment.

A Little Run

ON OUR FIRST SCOUTING TRIP, we planned to visit seventeen states in forty-eight days. Portland was an early stop in the itinerary. The mornings were chilly, below sixty degrees, so I ran with my face to the rising sun, following the sidewalk. First, an industrial stretch: a repair garage with two cars lifted on hoists, fast-food dives, a maple-furniture store. Smells of warming oil, grease vats, sawdust. The street was littered with scraps of newspaper. On the curb, the remains of a whole chicken nested on a pink paper napkin in an aluminum take-out tin. Next, a few commercial blocks of stores, boarded up: a delicatessen, a French bakery. Untrimmed vines and hedges, overgrown pine and Douglas fir, rhododendron and privet, untended flower beds, weeds—every green and wet thing sending out its roots like tentacles, taking back the part of the city no one cared about.

I had become a runner by accident. Lauren and I went for a walk one day, and on a whim I told her I wanted to see if I could run to a telephone pole a half-block away. "That's pretty far, Mother," she said.

Next thing I knew, I was running one, two, three miles. I was still teaching the special-ed kids then, and I used the time to mull over the challenges of their disabilities. But when Tommy and I started traveling, I was always getting lost. My problem is called prosopagnosia, from the Greek, *not knowing faces*, but also applies to having absolutely no sense of direction. In San Francisco, for instance, I found myself lost in Chinatown: dead ducks and pigs and rabbits hanging in the windows, strange smells, stares. No one who spoke English. People bargained, argued, in singsong tones. I ran on and on, deeper into a way of life I'd never seen. When I turned to go back, panic punched my stomach. I had no idea how to find our motel. I asked for directions from an older woman who shrugged and answered in a stream of Chinese.

The light was beginning to fade. Little paper lanterns, red, orange, yellow, blue, green, were glowing. "English?" I asked, again and again. Finally a young girl recognized my predicament, turned me around, told me what streets to look for. I vowed to always help anyone in trouble for the rest of my life. And I vowed from then on, wherever we went, to only run in a straight line—up this street, turn around, run back.

An hour later I found Tommy still at the pay phone at the Portland motel.

"You played a good game last night," he said, handing over the car keys. "How about lunch today to talk over your career plans?"

A few minutes later he returned to the van. "How'd it go?"

"Not good. Two fellows already have agents and two don't have phones. I can't talk to the good players—and the others, nobody wants. Not even me."

Pie

⟿

FEBRUARY 1986. TOMMY WAS DRESSED in his gray flannel suit, much too heavy for Texas in the spring, but I'd stopped telling him what to wear. We drove to Crockett, a small town named after Davy, the famous scout, soldier, and politician, population about five thousand.

"Don't tell me I don't take you to some of the finest places in the United States," he said. "I could even get you one of those raccoon hats here."

My son had had one, I told him. "He wore it every day and to bed at night."

"I used to play Peter Pan with my brother, but he got mad when I kept making him be Tinkerbell."

"And he's still lending us all this money?"

Tommy pulled up to a wooden, one-story house. "Well, wish me luck. And you be careful where you jog." A quick kiss and he was gone.

The only straight line I could find for my run was at the edge of town along the highway. A sixteen-wheel semi roared by so closely it blew my hat off. I rushed after it and scurried back to the berm. The hills were rolling and soft, covered with tall long-needled pines. Green water idled in swampy gullies. People waved, driving by, at what I supposed was a curiosity: a white woman jogging in ninety-one percent humidity.

Back at the van I collapsed on the running board. Three crows flew by. Across the street was a pair of old house trailers. A young man rode a little green mower back and forth. On the stoop of one trailer was an older man with his pant legs rolled up sipping beer. A skinny woman came out to converse with passengers in a car that stopped by.

Some looked over at our van from time to time. Lady, our cat, had stretched out for a nap on the couch.

At the end of his appointment Tommy escorted Isaiah out of the house.

"Happy to meet you, ma'am," he said, reaching through the window. A shy, deferential boy, he took my hand in his gently.

"Tommy's told me what a good player you are."

"Ah, I ain't so good. Both my brothers better than me."

"Don't let him fool you, Joanne," Tommy said, patting Isaiah on the back. "He's going to be one of the top players before long."

As we drove off I could see him in the rearview mirror, standing in the road, watching the van become a memory.

"Have other agents been talking to him?" I asked.

"Some. Not too many."

"Do you think he'll sign?" But I already knew that Tommy didn't work that way, pushing kids to close a deal.

"I just told him to let me help him for a while. I have to do it my way. It's really his older brother Gerald who's the best at this point, but his younger brother has a chance, too."

Our next stop was an old clapboard house with a wide front porch and rickety chairs out front. I rolled down all the windows in the van and opened the doors. A few minutes later, Tommy was back.

"Richard's mom insists you come in. She wants to meet you. When I told her you were out here she had a fit."

"I'm in my running clothes and all sweaty." I groaned and followed.

The temperature had risen. The house was sweltering and smelled of apples and cinnamon and perspiration.

Gloria took my hand. "I don't want you sittin' in no truck, hot as it is."

"I'm all a mess. I didn't want to intrude."

"You looks just fine, child. Meet my son, Richard."

Our new prospect was tall, handsome, muscular. His eyes were best: kind and trusting.

Two lattice-crust pies were cooling on the window sill.

"This my boy's last day home, so I made his favorite. He leave for the minor league camp in Columbus, Georgia, in the morning," Gloria said. "I guess you already knows that, though, and here I am telling you." She laughed. Her bosom rose and fell, and I wondered how many children must have felt comfort pressed against it.

We sat in overstuffed chairs in front of a large TV. A *Dallas* rerun was on, and Gloria and I talked about JR's wickedness. A yellow cloth on the back of my chair kept sliding off.

"That just for their curls so they don't get the chair all greasy, honey." She told me about losing her husband four years before to a massive heart attack. He'd been a coach, and then an elementary teacher in town when the schools were integrated. Thirty-seven years old.

"Don't know why black mens seems to die so young, like they tired of living." Gloria swept a paper fan across her face, staring into the distance. "He was the onliest man I ever loved. I just now beginning to believe he be gone."

She had five children and no means of support other than cleaning houses and taking in laundry. I admired the pictures of her family on the mantle and looked over a scrapbook of Richard's sports clippings.

"How did you pick baseball, Richard?" Tommy was pacing.

"I didn't have no trouble about that. I always like baseball the best. My brother, he better at football."

"That older boy ain't been nothing but a heartache to me," Gloria said, leaning toward me confidentially. "Got into drugs when his father died. He been in jail once already. The first time, I moves heaven and earth to help my children, but the second time they gets into trouble, it up to them to get out of it. I couldn't do nothin' about him. We all try. I take him to the preacher, and he no help neither. Not like Richard here. He always been a good boy. I could cry myself to sleep nights if I didn't have Richard."

"I have three children, and my youngest daughter has a lot of problems, too," I said. "I took her to a psychiatrist finally after the police called to say they'd picked her up at the mall, standing in the fountain collecting the coins people had tossed into it. She'd spent all her money and needed bus fare home, she said. Now we know it's schizrenia. We do the best we can. It must be hard with your husband gone."

"I just workin', workin', workin' night and day after my man pass. I guess I didn't spend enough time with the boy. How about a nice piece of apple pie? It cool off some now."

A younger boy walked into the kitchen to make himself a sandwich. He looked a little like Richard, fifty pounds heavier. The former special-ed teacher in me knew something was wrong with him.

"Mama, this bread stale," he said with a mouthful.

"What you mean, stale? No way it can be. I just buy it this morning."

"Maybe 'cause it taste like sto' bought bread. I likes yours better."

"I bakes two pies. What you want from me? I didn't have time to make no bread. Just eat what's there and stop your complaining.

But those pies for these nice folks and Richard. Don't you touch 'em now. Hear?"

"My mom, she make the best pie of anyone around," Richard said.

Gloria cut thick slices, pouring coffee for me and herself, milk for Tommy and Richard. "He my boy all right. Your sisters makes a good pie, too. I should know. I taught 'em."

Back in the living room, we settled again in front of the TV.

"Turn that thing off, Mom," Richard said. "My mom and her stories. She never want to miss them."

A girl in her teens joined us, carrying an infant.

"This here my older girl, Beverly. Say hello to these folks."

Next was a girl of about thirteen who smiled, but wouldn't look up at us. "Can I have some, Mama?" she whispered.

"This here's my fat girl," Gloria said laughing. "You don't need no pie. Wait and see if any left after the company goes." The girl hung around the edges of the room.

Tommy launched into his pitch: the slim chances of moving up in the minor leagues, the advantage of having someone representing him who cared about the person, not just the four-percent commission; how he wouldn't charge a penny until Richard was in the big leagues making $109,000 a year; how he'd get him shoes and batting gloves, and any other equipment he needed until then, and negotiate his contracts.

"Lordy, Lordy, one hundred…nine thousand dollars," Gloria said. "I don't even know what that mean. Six years back, Richard and his frien' couldn't play in high school 'cause they was black."

Tommy handed over the contract. "You don't need to sign now. Just look it over and think about it and when you feel ready to sign, you will."

"I don't need to think about it," Richard said. "I know when I like someone and sure do feel good about you and your wife. Let me have your pen."

"No, no, wait until you're ready. I don't want to rush you. I just want the chance to show you what a good job I can do."

Shut up and let him sign, I thought.

"Now you let my boy sign that there contract, Mr. Tommy. He know when he ready, and he ready now. No need to think about nothin'."

Four hours had passed. We were exhausted, but excited as kids as we left in the van. Our first contract!

"Everyone loves you right away," Tommy said. "You know how to make friends. Will you marry me now that I'm on my way to being rich and famous?"

"Let's get some Chinese food and I'll think about it," I said, kissing him.

Richard would make it to Double-A, graduate from college, marry, and work in a bank. And although Tommy would never make a dime representing him, that night we felt grateful for all of it: our fingers, entwined, Gloria and her pie, and her young son, alive with talent and hope.

A Dubious Talent

HAVE I EVER TOLD TOMMY how much I admired elevator operators when I was young? The fine department stores in Pittsburgh still employed them in the fifties, smartly uniformed men or women paid to do nothing more than ask "Floor, please?" and press the right buttons and keep the doors from closing on customers before they were out of the car. The risk of failure in a job like that was nearly zero, which seemed very appealing as a first-grade teacher.

My mother: she was one of four, raised poor and Catholic in a small coal-mining town in Charleroi, Pennsylvania. Her father, a glass-blower from Germany, was hit and killed by a street car in his forties. My father: he was one of twelve, a rebellious, resentful son, from a prominent Jewish family in Pittsburgh. His father, a philanthropist, was president of his synagogue. My father was a playboy and a gambler; my mother was his *shiksa* and, eleven years after their marriage, an alcoholic.

You could say I was an only child with survival stories on both sides, doted upon in that way that grooms children who excel at pleasing others. For my father, the grass *was* always greener elsewhere, and we moved often. (When I was in that Chevy van with Tommy, at least the ballpark lawns were all the *same* green, and our home moved with us.) By seventh grade, I had attended eight different schools, always that "new girl" who took the empty desk in mid-semester. But I was very good at making friends—just like when we hit the road to find players who needed agents, and just like now, decades later. Tommy knows me: I'm at my best at cocktail parties where I don't know anyone at all—a dubious talent that made me an excellent candidate for the job of a pretend wife-and-secretary to a pretend baseball agent.

Floor, please?

For the longest time, it seemed the only direction we were going was down.

A Mishap

HOW WE MET: PITTSBURGH, 1975. The phone rang. My friend Jackie had been playing tennis. "The ball hit me on the nose. I'm sure it's broken."

Jackie was not what you'd call a great athlete; great shopper, yes, great friend, yes, great tennis player, no.

"Don't be silly. You can't break your nose that way."

"It hurts and looks bent to one side."

"You'd know if it were broken."

"Please, please come to the doctor with me."

"Jackie, this is silly, but I'll pick up you up in ten minutes."

Such a hypochondriac, I thought.

She ran to my car clutching a paper towel with a cube of ice over her nose, still wearing her short tennis dress that, frankly, showed off her legs to perfection.

"Let me see."

"There's nothing to see. It's broken inside," she said, lifting the towel gingerly.

"What doctor?"

We drove to Dr. Busis's Oakland office. The waiting room was filled with patients reading magazines. Another overbooked physician.

Ugh. But Jackie was also his friend, so likely our wait would be… trimmed.

Before she was called in for the exam she introduced me to a young man, Tommy Tanzer.

"You know his mother, Joan. I can't believe you never met Tommy."

Jackie was still holding the paper towel over her nose. Then her number came up, and she left Tommy and me sitting next to each other on a plastic sofa with Muzak playing in the background. I tried to show polite interest, as anyone would do when meeting the grown child of a friend. He wore jeans, cowboy boots, and a cropped, brown leather jacket.

"I know your mother, your brother, your sister, and your father, but I've never met you."

He was short and dark with an interesting face: high cheek bones and brown eyes that had a certain sparkle to them. His dark brown hair was—rather long. He was neither handsome nor homely. Cute, maybe. I noticed the lips: full, sensuous.

"I really shouldn't be here. I came back from graduate school in Texas where I quit because I didn't like being told what my opinion should be about oil and everything else. The L.B.J. School of Public Affairs… I was supposed to have the operation last Monday for my deviated septum. Then it got cancelled because the doc thought I was on drugs, and here I am…back in his office waiting. And waiting."

"Were you?"

"What?"

"On drugs?"

"You know, maybe a little bit, nothing serious, just pot." He grinned up from under his black cap.

We talked like…old friends, but most of the time I couldn't understand what Tommy was saying. The conversation flew by me like a jet plane taking off.

I know he's speaking English, but for some reason I don't understand a word he's saying. Maybe if I listen more carefully I'll be able to follow this conversation.

When I questioned him about something, he'd pause and then make perfect sense of it. It was, I realized, as if he were ten minutes ahead of me.

For some reason I still don't understand I found myself telling him that I was going to leave Pittsburgh and move to Utah somewhere near Robert Redford's Sundance Resort in the Uintahs. I'd read about it in a magazine and liked the pictures of Robert wearing a fringed, suede jacket and cowboy hat, riding his horse through aspen groves in autumn and skiing in the brilliant sunshine in winter. I would get a job teaching school there and buy a little cabin in the mountains that I would never leave.

"Me, too," Tommy said. "I'll go. There's nothing here for me. Just tell me when you're ready."

Five minutes. Ten minutes. Maybe a half hour had passed.

Jackie was back. "Well, it's not broken."

I looked up, laughing. "What did he say?"

"I just told you. It's not broken." Jackie tossed her head.

"Good. I told you so." I stood to leave.

"I don't need to hear about how awful my tennis game is," she said, but even she had to chuckle.

Tommy tagged along as we left the doctor's office.

"Don't you still have an appointment?" I said.

"I've waited long enough. I have to get out of here." He shrugged.

"I practice medicine without a license," I said. "I'll operate."

"It's a deal," he said and plopped his cap on my head.

"Count me out," Jackie said. "I hate the sight of blood."

We were at my car. I handed over Tommy's hat. Jackie settled into the passenger seat.

"Glad to have met you," I said over my shoulder, but Tommy was still there, leaning into the window on the driver's side. He reached in and shook my hand, formally.

"Glad to have met you, too."

"What nice manners," Jackie said as we pulled away. "His mother will be proud when I tell her."

About That Cap

HIS MOTHER BROUGHT IT HOME from Greece when she and Poppy went on a trip. He was eighteen, maybe nineteen. He began to wear it all the time. His mother complained.

I'd never thought to ask him about it before now. "I didn't have a pompadour," is how he put it. With the hat covering his receding hairline, he could keep the back long and disguise the early signs of baldness.

Forty years later, he still wears that kind of hat, some wool, others lighter, gray, black, navy.

When we met he was wearing that cap, the Greek fisherman's cap, and heavy brown leather boots with the hems of his jeans tucked in. He looked to me like someone who was a free-thinker—and he was. It never occurred to him, he said, that there was anything wrong with falling in love with a woman seven years younger than his mother.

Mutah

MY MOTHER'S MOTHER, JOSEPHINE SCHIGET née Yeager, left Austria as a young girl with her husband, Henry. He was looking for work as a glass blower, and my grandmother's brother, John, knew there was a glass factory in Charleroi, Pennsylvania. On the way to America, Josephine gave birth to her first child, Adele, in the town that was still known as Constantinople, Turkey. How frightened she must have been.

Josephine once told me about the day their ship was docked, minutes away from disembarking. Henry was ashore. What would she do if he didn't return? She stood by the railing with her newborn searching the crowd. Illiterate. Didn't speak English. What would become of her in New York?

At the last minute Henry hurried up the gangplank. I imagine him disheveled and a little drunk. Probably he was drunk, according to my father, which might explain how he got himself killed by that streetcar on the way to visit his mother years later.

My parents' marriage and my birth were kept a complete secret from my father's side of the family. The disgrace, after all, of marrying a non-Jew. So Josephine took me in and cared for me from the time I was a newborn. She was my *mutah*.

One day my Aunt Adele said to my mother, "When are you going to bring your kid home?" The arrangement had been for three months, after all, not three *years*.

After the day my mother and father claimed me, it seemed to me that when Mutah visited, she would sit in a chair and look at me with sad eyes.

Lock 4

IN THE BEDROOM UPSTAIRS I drifted out of sleep like dandelion fluff floating on the wind. The raggedy edge of the dark-green window shade held back the sun, but one ripped corner let a golden splotch of light through, and it fell on the wall above my crib. I reached for it. A fly lit on my foot, its touch like the brush of an eyelash. I watched it explore my toes, laughed at the tickle. Under my pillow lay a crumpled white paper bag holding a few soft, sugary orange slices, a votive from my grandma to keep during my nap.

The door creaked open. I watched her head peer around it. A gray head, a smile.

"You up?"

These were the Depression years, the early thirties in the town of Charleroi, where my grandmother's two-story house on a hill overlooked Lock 4 on the Monongahela River. My mother, a teller in a bank, earned twenty dollars a week; my father, selling life insurance, made considerably less. They visited every weekend, no matter what the weather was like.

I thought they were nice, this woman I called Torie, short for Victoria, and this man I called Daddy. But the woman I loved, the woman I called Mommie, was the sun and moon of my life.

Late afternoons she dressed me in my freshly polished, white high-top shoes and a pastel-colored cotton dress, took my hand in her big, strong one, and we'd walk through the kitchen door, letting the sagging screened door slam behind us. Sometimes we climbed to the top of the hill to sit at the edge before the gravel-covered road began, looking down at the white frame house and the river below. A horizontal shelf of fractured gray stone became my private staircase with steps that fit my feet just so. Clinging to her hand, I climbed up and down, up and down, the granite levels. Sometimes we sat on the grassy slope and tied necklaces of white clover and hunted for those with four green leaves instead of three, for luck. Once I got into poison ivy, and my grandma had to scrub my legs with vinegar and a stiff, hard brush. It stung, but I didn't cry.

Twice a week we walked down the road to the paved street to buy a crusty loaf of Italian bread at the sweet-smelling bakery in the middle of the block.

My grandma—who I would come to understand was not my mommie, who was also known as Mutah—never baked bread, but she killed her own chickens for soup and gave me the feet for toys. I walked them across the blue-and-white checkered oilcloth on the kitchen table. We plucked the feathers, collecting them in cloth bags to make pillows. Her German shepherd, Boy, watched us work. She smoked a pipe sometimes, filled with tobacco from Prince Albert in a can.

Often we walked to her friend's house, Mrs. Mitchaloti's. The two older ladies let me sit with them at the great round dining table covered with a white, lacy cloth while they each sipped a glass of homemade red cherry wine. Mrs. Mitchaloti would pour a little glass for me sweetened with a teaspoon of sugar. I sat in the high-backed chair, holding my glass as the women did and listening, not to the words, but to the hum of their voices. My feet far off the floor, I turned in my chair to gaze at the tall, dark mahogany china closet with a glass door protecting the treasures within: ladies made of porcelain china with long, ruffled dresses and fans, painted many colors.

When the visit was over, my grandma took my hand in hers, and we slowly walked home down to the middle of the hill.

At night I would lie in her large brass bed with all the quilts and pillows, watching as she took out her big hairpins and let down what she called a *plait* to hang halfway down her back. My grandma didn't know how to read, but she listened to the soap operas on the radio, and she'd recap the latest episode for me at bedtime. I snuggled up to her warm, ample body, held rapt by her words as other children might, hearing fairy tales. She told me the stories with great expression, oohing and ahhing over some girl who "got in the family way." I didn't know what that meant, but it sounded intriguing. Together, our imaginations thrived.

I remember a picture she drew for me on white paper: a mailman ascending straight vertical and horizontal lines, representing the porch steps, with a bag of mail on his shoulder. He always had a letter for me in his hand. We made up the letter and the sender.

Sometimes my grandma sang me songs in German in her deep, masculine voice. Like a star of the opera, she puffed up her chest and belted out "Du, Du Liegst Mir im Hersen" or recited little verses she and her brothers and sisters once sang outside the kitchen window to tease their mother before they ran away into the fields.

She told me stories about when she was a little girl and how she worked with her father in a glass factory in the Old Country. In order to work, every glass blower had to have a small child for a helper to gather the pieces of glass.

"I had to jump up on a little"—here a pause while she groped for the English word for *platform*—"table and pick up all the glass my father blew and put it in my basket before I brought it back down to him. That's why I never got to go to school and learn to read and write." Ashamed that she signed her name with an X, she eventually learned to scrawl like an overgrown child, JOSEFA SCHIGET, a feat of which she was quite proud.

Before we went to sleep my grandma said her rosary, slipping the little black beads on the silver chain through her gnarled fingers and moving her lips. I didn't know if the prayers were in English or German. I pretended to say the rosary, too, with my imaginary beads, sliding my fingers back and forth.

On weekends we walked all the way to the highway and sat on a low stone wall in front of someone's house to wait for Torie and Daddy to visit.

One day they came and packed my things and put me in the car and slammed the door shut. I looked out the window down at the house and river and the screen door and we drove away, and I never forgave them.

Pagan Love Song

I ALWAYS THOUGHT THAT SONG was called "Tahitian Skies," which, as it turned out, is an instrumental tune. But I remembered my father singing to me, *Native hills are calling, to them we belong.* Search Google on *that* line, as a friend did recently, and up pop the lyrics for "Pagan Love Song," written by Nacio Herb Brown and Arthur Freed, and a 1927 vintage recording comes warbling through my friend's computer speakers. My father would have been eighteen that year.

> Come with me where moonbeams light Tahitian skies
> And the starlit waters linger in our eyes
> Native hills are calling, to them we belong
> And we'll cheer each other with the pagan love song

I wept when I heard it—eighty years had passed. But why would that song have appealed to a Jew from Pittsburgh who had never laid eyes on a palm tree much less a tropical island? Did my father have to consult Merriam Webster concerning the word *pagan*?: "One who has little or no religion and who delights in sensual pleasures and material goods; an irreligious or hedonistic person." And if so, did he find some reassurance in learning, at last, that he actually belonged to some tribe other than the one that gathered at the synagogue?

Max Azen, his father, the synagogue's president and benefactor, would have snorted his disdain at the suggestion: *Pagan? What you are is a schmuck*, which roughly translated means a penis. (In Yiddish the word for *jeweler* was *schmuckler*, a man who considers his genitalia his jewels.)

This part is not a memory someone implanted; it has to be my own: I am three or four and my father is singing to me: *And we'll cheer each other with the pagan love song.* The room was dark and I nestled against his hairy chest. I want to believe that he knew I was sad because they had taken me away from Mutah, that he was trying to comfort me.

A Blessed Virgin

MY HAPPIEST MEMORIES DATE TO the fourth and fifth grades. We had a house in Stanton Heights. A group of girls would walk to school every morning and back again after. At four o'clock I would change clothes, get a snack, and go out in the street to play until dinner. In summer we played until dark—Red Rover and Duck, Duck, Goose. I had a crush on a boy, Donald Yates.

"I'd like her except she's a Jew," he told someone. I'd never heard that was bad thing to be.

In truth I was half and half, which was worse in a certain way.

My parents said I could be anything I wanted, Catholic like my mother or Jewish like my father.

What if I didn't want to be anything?

When I was twelve I was sent to a Girl Scout camp in Cloudcroft, New Mexico, for two weeks. 1944. We were living in Texas to be near my father who was now in the army. I didn't know a soul. My trunk had been lost in transit. Someone loaned me a blanket as we sat around the fire pit the first night. When the conversation turned to religion I was nervous, but announced I was Jewish. No one had ever met one before. The girls felt my forehead for horns.

I found myself standing, saying what I believed, none of which had anything to do with the Christmas in July celebration that had been arranged. But I was picked to be the Blessed Virgin, wearing a white sheet and a blue veil. We proceeded slowly down the mountain trail to the dining hall. The baby Jesus was in my arms as I rode the donkey—amazing that I could sit astride it, having just given birth!—that kept company with a stable of horses.

One night we camped in the woods. I woke up about three or four in the morning and climbed to the top of a fire look-out. Sitting alone there in the dark I thought, *I don't belong anywhere. I'm all alone. I don't know who I am or where I belong.*

I had bad thoughts. If you had bad thoughts about someone, you were told you had to pray for forgiveness. I had a lot of bad thoughts about Betty Ann Mohn. She was blonde and pretty and the leader of the popular girls. They would pick on the unpopular ones like Pat Crowley who was fat and unattractive and shy. On the Girl Scout weekend Betty Ann had the girls break up pieces of a Baby Ruth bar to put in Pat's bed. At Bambi's direction, they pulled back the sheet. "Look, she made a poop!" Of course Pat ran off crying. I was too much of a coward to do anything about it. I was too scared that Betty Ann would turn her wrath on me. I stood there, I stared, and I didn't say a word. Of course I had bad thoughts about Betty Ann. And to this day…I'm ashamed I didn't speak up.

Back in school in Pittsburgh, the nuns were always trying to convert me. When we read biographies, I was given the *Biographical Memoirs of St. John Bosco*. In the class play, I was given the role of Mother Seton and almost fell into a religious calling because of the nun's habit. I felt so holy with the white cowl tucked against my face, the black skirt flowing around my heels, the wide sleeves enveloping my crossed arms, the heavy leather belt anchoring my waist, and the cross draped around my neck. Definitely a costume, but it put me in the mood and made the idea of being married to God and sacrificing my life for Him hugely appealing.

My questions got me in trouble, though. I asked why, if sex was only for procreation, did Catholics practice the rhythm method?

"Joanne, you need to pray for more faith."

I said I understood who the Father and Son were, but the Holy Ghost?

"Joanne, you need to pray for more faith."

This was around the time I'd asked my father about the meaning of life. We were standing in the tiny kitchen in our apartment on Hempstead Road. Through the window I could hear the sounds of children playing in the street. He leaned against the sink and smacked his lips as he spooned a can of grapefruit into his mouth. "Smarter people than you have tried to figure that out, so don't worry about it. Can you believe they can get these perfect segments into the can? Delicious."

But in class at the Rodef Shalom Temple I asked about life after death.

"No one knows. Read these writings on either side of the question and make up your own mind." Finally, an answer I could live with.

Solitaire

It doesn't make sense, really. I was already in the powder-blue gown with tulle around a low-cut neckline that I was wearing to the prom. She was sitting at the dining table playing solitaire when I asked her to paint my nails. Wouldn't I have done that before I got dressed? Did I just want her to notice me, to secure her undivided attention?

She tried, but the polish was all over my cuticles, slopped over the sides of my nail beds. She was very drunk. It was at that exact moment I said to myself, "You can never depend on your mother again. You're on your own."

Here's another thought: Maybe I realized she was drunk, so I set her up. Maybe I just needed to prove to myself what I already knew to be true.

She might have been wearing the solitaire diamond ring my father gave to her the day of the Normandy invasion. We were having breakfast at the counter of a diner in Texas before he was shipped overseas. I think I remember seeing a newspaper with a huge headline, but that could be my imagination. But I do remember her putting the ring on her finger, on her large right hand.

Fifteen-hands High

My mother had always had a voracious appetite for calamity, so it was no wonder that her drinking escalated after my father was shipped off to war. "He could be dead somewhere in Germany and we wouldn't even know," she'd say, her face stricken, if no letter from him had arrived that day.

I rode in a cab pool to my Catholic high school every morning but caught a trolley home in the evenings. The aroma of family dinners would wrap around me in the hallway outside of our apartment; our kitchen would be cold and dark as a cave. My mother's bedroom door would often be closed.

Reprieve came every weekend, and every day during the summer, at Milt Selznick's stable. In exchange for mucking stalls and oiling saddles and reins, I spent long happy hours under his tutelage on a palomino the color of spun gold he'd picked out for me. The horse was a bargain struck with my father who'd agreed to buy it for me if I agreed not to leave home to go to college.

Milt was charismatic but also a strict taskmaster and consummate professional, training riders and horses to race, hunt, jump, and perform dressage. Utterly devoted to the animals, he rejected the overtures of his cousin, David O. Selznick, the famous director, who wanted Milt to move to Hollywood to train animals for appearances in movies during a time when their welfare would have been at best a secondary consideration.

Of course I had crush on him; many of the young women at the stable did, and rumors of his involvement with a few of them provided a steady source of gossip. And while I could have become one of those he loved and left, I suppose, what I needed most at the time was a parent; two of them actually. I was blessed to have found him in my life.

The Housedress

I THINK ABOUT MY LIFE with Jack as my other life. All those dreams. I stood at the kitchen sink watching the leaves on our pin oaks turn gold in the fall, washing lettuce for our salad, cleaning fresh vegetables to accompany the leg of lamb, the rib roast, the chicken, the pork chops.

I loved our house, a greystone bungalow with a green slate roof. I'd walk into the dining room and see the sun shining through the window on a bowl of red apples on the table and think, *How lovely.* I believed I'd live in that house for decades to come; I planned on turning one of the three bedrooms into a nursery for grandchildren and the second bedroom into a guest room for my children and their spouses. We had a gardener, Al Seppi, who planted white petunias and red geraniums in the front yard, while I planted tulips along the backyard fence.

Some warm summer afternoons I would walk with the children up Linden Avenue, one child in the stroller, one walking beside it. We'd take the route Jack would take, driving home, hoping to meet him on the way. I loved wearing the "swirl" housedresses then in fashion, which wrapped around the front and were tied off on the side, something like some hospital gowns are now, but prettier, of course, with a V-neck and rickrack trim. They made me feel like a real housewife, mature, not the teenager some people thought I was. Whenever I answered the door in the housedress, though, the caller, usually a man, would ask if my daddy was home.

We seldom ran into Jack, though. He never, or hardly ever, came home before the children had eaten, been bathed, and put to bed. It never occurred to me to ask him to help, but I do remember him saying, "I really don't like little children. I'll pay more attention to them when they get older, around ten or so."

Eventually I had a full-time maid, Frances Clark. She was sixteen, maybe seventeen, when she came to work for me. I was twenty-three. We're still in touch all these years later. In fact, she met us the day we spread Jack's ashes around a tree in a tiny park near Forbes Field.

Gatsby's Tailor

OUR LIPS MADE SECRET SMILES and hinted at private passions. He tilted his head at the dance floor, him in his satin-lapelled tuxedo, me in my white crepe gown, embellished with silver beads around the cuffs and neck, its slim sheath of skirt slit up one side, flashing a stockinged leg and a silver pump. I wore the ring, a square emerald set between two kite-shaped diamonds, my tenth-anniversary present.

"Did you know that Larry has been having an affair, for years?"

"You're kidding," Jack said. "Why would *he* have an affair anyway? With all his money, he doesn't need to have an affair."

We swayed through the merengue. The country club had gone all out: spring tulips and daffodils, hyacinth and narcissus arrangements on tables. White linen. Candles flickering. White-gloved waiters and uniformed waitresses passing hors d'oeuvres on silver trays. Wives doused with Shalimar and Chanel. Long tables laden with cold shrimp and pâté foie gras and crab meat. Swans carved from ice as smooth as crystal. Platters of glistening black caviar, thick, white swirls of sour cream and chopped egg yoke, red and yellow tomatoes carved into roses. Molded salmon salad.

French doors opened onto terraces and the lush greens and fairways of the golf course. Couples with addresses not the same drifted out those doors into the moonlight.

"J & B on the rocks? And a white wine for the missus?" asked the bartender.

"Remember," I whispered, "You don't have to buy everyone a drink."

"What's the difference?" Jack said, turning away, taking a long sip of scotch.

"The difference is at the end of the month when you hand me the checkbook and the bills to pay and give the barely-keeping-our-heads-above-water lecture," I said.

"That *was* pretty funny when you wore your shower cap." He slipped away then to the high-stakes gin rummy game.

"Please don't play too late," I said, moving toward a circle of women friends.

I knew their lives, even if they didn't know mine: days in a flurry of activity. Getting everyone off to school and work in the mornings, planning the dinner menu with the maid, phoning service people to deliver groceries, arranging to have the TV fixed and the trees pruned, rushing to tennis or golf lessons, meeting for lunch or attending Ladies Hospital Aide meetings, hurrying home to chauffeur children to piano and ballet lessons or dentist appointments, then changing for dinner and having a martini or two with their husbands before company arrived, taking courses at the university, flying to New York to shop and see plays.

They spoke of their homes, their trips, their clothes, their children. The decorator, planning a white marble floor with diamond-shaped brass inserts for the foyer. The travel agent putting together the itinerary for a month-long trip to the Orient. The salesgirl from Linton's, calling about an Anne Klein dinner jacket trimmed with gold braid and colored stones. The admissions secretary writing to say that a six-year-old son had been accepted to Shadyside Academy that fall.

I said little, went to the bar for a refill.

Let's call him Granger. He was married and standing too close. "Dance?"

He guided me to the floor.

"Meet me for lunch?"

"Just lunch?"

"We can think about what's on the menu after we see how hungry we are."

"Why would I do that?"

"I appreciate you. You're alluring. Bored."

"You could say that about half the women in this room."

"I do."

We laughed.

Jack emerged from the locker room wearing a particularly broad smile, the one that said, *I lost*.

Time to go.

We waited in front of the clubhouse for the valet to bring the car.

"How much?" I said.

"A lot."

"How much?"

"Five hundred."

We drove on, silent, the dark roads sliding by. Clouds had moved in, obscuring the moon and the stars, as if the stage lights had been lowered.

"I wrote a check. It won't bounce until Tuesday."

"I have two hundred saved from my housekeeping expenses. You could have that."

He reached over, squeezed my hand, his handsome face full of trouble.

"Maybe I could rob a bank, pull an insurance scam."

"I could become a prostitute."

We pulled into the driveway of our lovely home in the wooded suburb where our bright and beautiful children slept with our prize-winning springer spaniel and live-in maid.

"We can't afford all this. We're running with the wrong crowd," I said.

"I've known these people since I was a little boy. Who'd we be friends with? Al, the bartender?"

"He's a nice man. At least he doesn't make passes at your wife."

We slept on opposite sides of the bed for what little remained of the night, hugging the edges of the mattress, our backs turned against one another, careful not to touch. A hard rain drummed on the roof.

Sunday morning, after Jack left for his golf game, I took the shears from my sewing basket. First I sawed through a sleeve of his tuxedo jacket, then I sliced the trousers, snipping them in two, right up to the crotch.

Let's see how he does pretending to be the Great Gatsby now. Miss Daisy Buchanan has left the building.

A Good Sport

THAT NIGHT TOMMY AND I parked the van in an orange grove. The trees formed a thick bower over us, obscuring the sky. The air was sweet, redolent with the smell of ripe fruit. We sat on the bumper of the van eating an orange Tommy had picked for us to share, juice dripping from our hands, smeared on our mouths. The next day we had an appointment with David Carlucci and his family at a restaurant.

David's mother was a plump, short woman in a shapeless dress printed with flowers. She was probably younger than I was, but her hair was graying, braided and pinned into a bun at the nape of her neck.

"I made Tommy Lasorda a big pan of spaghetti and meatballs," she said. "Italians like to eat."

"I bet it was delicious," I said. What could I make him should the circumstances present themselves? Matzah-ball soup and chopped liver?

Tommy delivered his usual spiel about what he could do for David. I tried to charm his mother, asking about David playing baseball when he was little. David's father didn't have much to say. David excused himself and went to the restroom.

His uncle took the opportunity to ask Tommy in a booming voice, "What do you want with a bum like him?"

Dead silence. But I knew Tommy. He was a good talker.

"I see a lot of potential. He has drive and desire. That's what a player needs."

Tommy had studied David's stats; the problem was they'd been accumulated in Great Falls, Montana, in the Pioneer League, considered rookie ball, lower than even A-ball, which was four levels below the major leagues.

"The guy can't hit. He's my nephew, sure, but he can't hit," said the uncle.

"A lot of guys mature late," Tommy said. "Players don't reach their prime until they're twenty-nine in baseball. David's only twenty-three."

"What's going on?" David said, sliding back into his chair.

"Nothing. Tommy just told us a joke."

Poor David. He only made the Dodgers's minor league. He really couldn't hit. But years later he got a job as a bullpen catcher in Boston, where he was from, for the Red Sox.

That's how you make orange juice out of lemons.

Bums

⤚ح

I STILL LOVE TO WATCH fielding plays on TV, a player throwing himself on the ground to make a catch.

I love their fearlessness. I love how they love the game.

I love the crack when the wood hits the ball, how a player thanks God when he gets a home run.

I love the fans, even the ill-behaved: *You bum! You couldn't hit the side of a barn! Get a bushel basket, you butterfingers! You puss arm! Go back to where you came from!*

Where else can a shoe salesman behave like that in front of his son?

But watching minor league games night after night? Sometimes I'd be praying that the game wouldn't go into extra innings. I wanted to go home, even if home was a motorhome—and I'd feel the same way years later when we could afford motels.

It was a Dodgers game. Tommy and I only had one position player in the game, Dougie Dascenzo in centerfield. I paid attention when he batted, but in between I read. Dougie would play six years in the majors then become the minor-league coordinator for the Chicago Cubs after years with the San Diego Padres. I should have appreciated his love, and his fans' love, of the game.

An older lady came up and screamed at me. "At a baseball game?! How dare you read a book!"

Guess I found out who the real bum was.

A Liberated Woman
(not yet)

~~6~~

WHEN I WAS ENROLLED AS a creative-writing major at the University of Pittsburgh in 1949, tuition was $10.50 per credit. An entire semester cost $150. My father had started at Duquesne University but had dropped out in the first semester saying he'd gotten hurt playing football—all five-foot-four of him. My mother had never been to college.

"What do you mean you're taking creative writing?" my mother said. "What would you do if your husband got sick and you had to earn a living? You get back there and learn something so you can support a family."

In those days women could be secretaries, teachers, or nurses. Being a secretary sounded awful. I wouldn't have minded nursing, but I'd heard nurses were fast with doctors—and I didn't trust myself.

I became a teacher.

I married at nineteen.

I had a baby at twenty, twenty-two, and twenty-six.

It took me years to earn my first degree. Then I found out that I needed twelve more credits as a "punishment" for not having taught during those years I was having children. When at last I had my teaching certificate, I put my name on a list for substitute teachers.

When I finally got a full-time job, I had to ask my husband permission to take it. At first Jack was insulted. He wasn't working, was "between investments," was bringing in $50 a month—but this job of mine was a blow to his manhood. I had to promise him everything would be the same, nothing would change. Yes, I would still go to the dry cleaners. Yes, I would still shop for groceries and make five-course dinners every night. Yes, I would still get the kids ready for school. He finally agreed.

I taught a first-grade class in a Pittsburgh blue-collar district, enduring a principal who said to my face, "These women whose husbands work and make a perfectly good living and still decide to teach make me sick." I earned $5,495 a year.

We went away with another couple and our children over New Year's weekend. Jack lost that much betting on football over the course of three days.

You Think That's Bad: Two

WHAT I THOUGHT (ON THE rare occasions we did have sex): *Please don't let him lose his hard-on,* which, if it happened, I believed was my fault.

Because what he said was this:

> "You're not fat, just chunky. Legs like tree trunks." And my rear end was "like Roy Campenella's," the pro baseball player.

> "You're not tall enough."

> "You have too much hair down there." (So I would sit on the toilet seat with the bathroom door locked, snipping away with cuticle scissors.)

And this:
                                       "You're too wet." (I didn't know at the time that most men might find that, well, encouraging. And what could I do, anyway, sprinkle flour on my private parts?)

What I know now, thanks to psychology: unhappy people tend to project their unhappiness onto others.

Kick Off

OUR FIRST CHILD WAS BORN on the last day of November 1952.

It's not yet dawn when my water breaks. I have a suitcase packed; Jack dashes outside to shovel snow from the porch steps. We stop on the way to the hospital for breakfast. I know better than to eat anything; Jack has waffles and coffee.

"We're on the way to have a baby," he tells the waiter, scaring the poor guy half to death.

At that time the father wasn't allowed in the delivery OR, but there was Jack dressed in green scrubs with the obstetrician Dr. Meyers, a friend of his, who had bent the rules.

Jack stood at the edge of the gurney, looking down at me. So handsome! Suddenly his eyes filled with tears—I'd never seen him cry. Could we be any happier than at that moment?

When I was returned to my hospital room, Jack was already there, sitting in a chair in front of the TV.

"You made me miss the best football game of the season," he said.

And he wasn't joking.

Not Your Usual Minyan

IT WAS ON ANOTHER JULY day in Pittsburgh, a year after I'd met Tommy in the doctor's office, when my friend Jackie's father-in-law, Saul, died after a long illness. After the funeral and the interment at the cemetery, Jackie's mother-in-law sat *shiva* in her home. Cream cheese and lox and bagels were offered, along with hard-boiled eggs, the traditional food of mourning. A pauper's food, eggs. You wouldn't want to eat a fancy meal with, say, caviar, at this time, but you do need to do something that says, *Life will go on.* An egg, it has no opening, no beginning or end. It keeps going round and round. (Also the longer you boil the eggs, the tougher they get—like the Jews, some say.)

Jack had left work early to attend. We were separated by then, and I dreaded being in the same room with him, especially among friends who'd known us for years. That dubious talent of mine that carried me through parties with strangers worked just as well in this context. I helped serve food; I chatted. I did my best to ignore Jack, but I noticed Tommy, who joined the group of ten men, including my ex, for the minyan. Why ten?: Abraham argued with God when He wanted to destroy Sodom. Would He raze the town if there were a hundred good men? God said no. What if there were ninety? Eighty? Seventy? Sixty? Fifty? And so on, until God agreed that if Abraham could find ten good men…

As the ancient prayer went on, I had to laugh, watching Tommy. He closed his eyes and mumbled, but obviously didn't know a word of Hebrew. And instead of a *kippah*, he wore that same Greek cap I'd seen him in the day we'd met.

"He's a manufacturer's rep," Tommy's father told me, "for a line of furniture. His territory takes him all the way to North Carolina. He just started out, but he's doing well." I excused myself to get more coffee.

"Jack's telling everyone that his wife has just taken a sabbatical from marriage and will be back soon," Jackie whispered. Not likely. It had taken me five months to make up my mind to leave him after twenty-three years of his philandering and lies.

I could see Tommy's hands in his lap, small, almost feminine, the inflamed, bitten nails. He was an appealing boy, all the same.

Stakeout

You don't have to be much of a private eye when your philandering husband takes you on a tour to visit the apartment building of his former paramour.

This was during that three-year period when I thought we were reconciled, when I thought Gerry was in California. One day Jack didn't come home as expected and that sick feeling in my stomach started getting worse and worse. I felt overwhelming sadness. Everything seemed so black.

I drove to Gerry's place, parked out of sight and walked through the front door and up three flights of stairs. (Jack had even told me her apartment number, I suppose in the interest of full disclosure while in the throes of his remorse.)

I could hear a man's voice through the door. Jack? Then her voice. My heart splintered into shards as I slunk around the corner.

The visitor turned out to be a salesman of some sort. I know because I hid behind a pillar in the lobby and watched him leave—then her. She was tall, a redhead. She turned and looked back—not particularly beautiful. Did she see me? What did he see in her?

What?

Then Came Darren

I WASN'T IN LOVE WITH him. I loved my adulterous husband and that pain was bad enough.

I had an affair to punish Jack for his affairs.

I had an affair because my husband didn't enjoy sex with me.

I had an affair because the excitement from the intrigue and danger was better than feeling numb.

Jack was out of town that day. Darren and I were supposed to meet in the parking lot. He never showed up; I was furious.

Jack was the one who called that night to say Darren had committed suicide.

He had serious heart problems, serious money problems. Maybe for Darren, for a while, our affair was some kind of proof that life was still worth living. I'll never know. But this I do know: he didn't kill himself over me. Yet, I have lived with the shame of it all for so long— the shame of the affair mixed up with the shame of not confronting my failing marriage head-on for far too long.

The shame of just how selfish I could be.

The Netherland
(from an old diary)

July 3, 1974

I'm drinking a scotch and water. It's very hot and humid, about ninety-two degrees, and the air conditioning is barely working. Outside the wind is blowing—hot and sticky—leaves are moving, sunlit. I can hear children's voices from the neighbor's pool next door. I'm reading Jaws, *a good, fast, summer-read.*

I'm trying to get my head together, as they say.

I don't know where I'm going or what direction to choose. I'm flying in fragments! Little pieces of me are scattered all over the ground. Self-pity wells up inside of me and I hate it. I thought I had all the answers, simple, straight-forward, down the middle, and now I'm bitter and angry. Good was good. Now good is schumucky. I'm such a fool, the asshole of the world. I've been knocking myself out for so long and for what? I don't know and I don't stop. I don't even know what I want.

Everything I do is for effect. In fact I just read this over to see if it would make a nice impression. I don't even know who I am. I've been playing a role for so long—mother, wife, teacher, homemaker, in with the in-crowd, bright, with-it...I don't know what I like! Maybe that's where I should start.

What do I like? Skiing, swimming, the outdoors, lovemaking, food, cigarettes, ballet, scotch, sleep, snow. I really love snow, grass, dogs, horses, all animals, air, storms, ocean, stones, sand, clay, fireplaces, Frank Lloyd Wright's Falling Water, *clothes, baths, clean sheets, my pillow.*

I'm afraid I'm going to turn out to be like my mother after all.

August 1974

I feel compassion for Jack. He's truly sorry in his heart and wants to make up for all the years but doesn't know how. He wants an instant return on his investment, so he can't offer the gradual, patient, giving of self that builds a relationship. He becomes overbearing, obnoxious, then talks baby-talk and expects me to be appreciative. Instead he makes an ass of himself. The truth lies somewhere in the middle: he's not the selfish hedonist or the jerky asshole but something in between—warped but also good and generous. And selfish. Taking what he wants and when he's sated, sorry if anyone else got hurt.

I want to forgive him, but I can't. My heart cries out in pain for the child I was, for all I gave, and how little I got in return. I seek revenge, but that demeans me. I try to forgive and count the good things, which are many, but I'm too small and mean a person. What do I do?

How do I get it all together?

I must come to a decision.

The Netherland is killing us all.

Batter Up

I'LL ADMIT IT: I LOVED baseball when I was young. I was thirteen. My grandfather's business, Max Azen Furs, owned a box on the third-base side of Forbes Field, which made me popular with my girlfriends, who were all for ditching school in Oakland and walking a few blocks to go take in a game. Naturally a big part of the attraction was the Pittsburgh Pirates players themselves, handsome, older men: Elbie Fletcher, Rip Sewell, Hank Greenberg, Ralph Kiner. I looked older than I was back then; Clyde McCullough tried to pick me up once in the lobby of the Hotel Webster Hall. I knew better than to let it go too far.

What I didn't know then was that baseball players are boys trying to *act* like men. All their lives they've been stars, starting with Little League when they found themselves better than their peers, able to run faster, throw farther, make contact with the ball more often. Their dads were early mentors, avid fans, some dreaming about their sons turning pro. A few would actually make it into A-ball, hoping to climb the ladder to Double- and Triple-A.

The problem was that only four percent ever make it to the Big Show. The problem was, Tommy would only start getting paid as their agent if they got that far.

Like me, Tommy had always loved baseball. He'd spend long weekends reading baseball stats, which I thought was a complete waste of time. He was teaching in the Park City, Utah, school system back then, and Tommy being Tommy, he got himself embroiled in pay-raise negotiations for the teachers in his district. That's how it all began. That's when Tommy decided he was going to be an agent.

The Utah Education Association rep at the time was Kevin Barton, a caricature of a man on the make, an anomaly, to say the least, as a Mormon. Too-much-information alert: everyone knew he'd wrap a washcloth around his penis and safety-pin it in place to impress women. He wore his shirt open to the waist—meaning he wasn't a fan of wearing his temple garments. A gold chain nestled against his hairy chest.

"Kevin, sit up and put your legs together. We've got work to do," Tommy hissed. "And button up your shirt. No one wants to see all that."

At this particular meeting Tommy laid out his demands. "What we want for the teachers, the bus drivers, the cafeteria workers, the aides, everyone, is a thirty-percent raise."

Cecil Thomas, the Park City superintendent, sat up. "That's ridiculous. The most any teachers have ever gotten is four percent." It was widely known he'd raised salaries for former superintendents from $39,283 to $160,000 a year, but most teachers didn't have the fight in them that Tommy did.

Cecil's British accent charmed most. Yet, in spite of his conversion to Mormonism, he was known to drink and smoke. When he wasn't posing as a model educator, he womanized.

"That would make us the first," Tommy said.

Mouths gaped. The other committee members swung their heads back toward Cecil.

"We would also like to have our insurance raised by $1,500 per person and memberships for everyone at the Prospector Health Club. You know, healthy teachers would be an asset—fewer sick days, big savings."

The meeting was adjourned by nine a.m.

Cecil called Tommy to his district office the next day after school. "What do you want?" he demanded.

"I told you," Tommy said.

"What do you want personally? You can't think you'll get this settlement."

"I don't want anything."

"Looks like the teachers will be going on strike then."

"We're not striking," Tommy said. "We won't alienate the parents. We'll work without a contract as long as we have to."

"Everyone has a price."

"We have these photographs of you coming out of Walmart with the first-grade aide—and some others—that wouldn't be good for your reputation." Tommy slapped a manila envelope on the desk and left.

By the fall, at the end of negotiations, the teachers had gotten a twenty-three percent raise, better insurance, and those health-club memberships. Then the grumbling began: *You said we'd get a thirty-percent raise.*

"That's not how you negotiate," Tommy said. "You ask for more than you expect and then come down. Everyone thinks they've won."

"And the photos?"

"A deal is a deal. We gave Cecil the negatives."

"I'm making $19,000 a year for this?" Tommy said to me. "I could be doing this for baseball players and making decent money."

By the next summer, we'd quit our jobs and bought the blue Chevy van.

A Reading Lesson

THE SUMMER OF 1975. PITTSBURGH. I was alone in the house. Lauren had gone to summer camp again, and again Richard worked as a camp counselor there.

This was my time to myself before my teaching job started again. I had finished an exhausting six-week summer school class in the diagnosis and remediation of reading problems at the University of Pittsburgh. My friend Steffie and I were supposed to play golf, but the day dawned cool and rainy. I found myself relieved when we cancelled our game. It meant I would have time to do some things around the house. My home of twenty years meant so much to me, maybe even more after Jack and I separated. I leaned the ladder against the lamp post on the front lawn and climbed up to change the light bulb. And, while I was at it, I had a damp cloth in hand to wipe down the lamp's glass panels.

The phone was ringing inside the house.

"Damn." I scrambled down the ladder. It could be one of my children.

"Hi, this is Tommy. Remember me?"

"The boy with the hat at the doctor's office." *Boy*, I said, on purpose.

"Someone told me you were a reading specialist."

"I'm working toward it. I normally teach first grade."

"I have a reading problem."

"I find that hard to believe. I mean, you've made it to graduate school."

"I do. I really do. I was wondering if I could come over and talk to you about it, maybe get some help?"

Hmm. *Really?* "I'll be here for the rest of the afternoon," I said, thinking of Mrs. Robinson—from the movie. I found myself checking the mirror, putting on lipstick, combing my hair. What do we mean when we say, *I found myself*…doing this, doing that? Does it mean we are living outside of ourselves for a while, the bodies and minds we think we know so well?

My eyes looked very green owing to the old green tee shirt I had on. I didn't go so far as to change out of my faded jeans. *Maybe they make me look younger.*

I went back outside to finish work on the lamp post.

Then Tommy was walking towards me in the cul-de-sac, that cap on his head, wearing a denim jacket and carrying a newspaper folded under his arm. He had a jaunty stride. I had to laugh. *Hullo, Dustin Hoffman.*

He steadied me, taking my hand as I climbed down, and carried the ladder into the garage.

"Can I get you something? A Diet Coke? Iced tea? *(Or me?)*

"Sure."

"Which?"

He was self-assured and shy, too. It took *chutzpah* to go visit a friend of his mother's with that aggressive twinkle in his eye. Maybe it wasn't true that the meek inherited the earth. I mean, I'd been meek for twenty-three years and look where it had gotten me.

I poured two Diet Cokes and set them on the glass-topped table in the kitchen. He sat down in the chair next to me. I could feel something, a tension, an awakening, in my stomach.

He spread the *New York Times* out on the table. Afternoon sun broke through the clouds and shone on the charcoal-hued brick of the kitchen floor.

"I'm such a slow reader. Everything takes me too long."

"I'm not Evelyn Wood. I've had one day's training in speed-reading and…I'm a slow reader myself."

I told him the basic principles of speed reading: it was a matter of practice. "I hate to read fast. I like to linger over the words, reread a passage that I like, turn back in a book, but of course, if I were reading the news…I should read faster."

"How do you do that?"

His eyes broadcast an innocence that I didn't feel.

"The first thing reading teachers have to determine is whether the student is intellectually impaired or in the normal range. This past summer in grad school I learned how to give a rather simple I.Q. test, the Slosson, and I haven't been able to find people to practice on. I could give you the test one day, if you like."

"Then you'd find out I'm not too smart."

I smiled. "I don't think so."

The afternoon darkened again as rain clouds moved in and thunder rolled in the distance. Yeah, good thing the golf game was cancelled.

I brought out oatmeal cookies and fruit that neither of us touched.

I went to my room and came back with my riding spurs. English spurs with dulled points, not the jangly western style. I had saved them along with my boots and riding crop and black velvet hat from those way-back days when I'd had my own horse.

"What are these for?

"I don't know. It just seems you should have them."

"Are you sure? How do they work?"

I knelt beside the table to wrap the leather straps around Tommy's boots.

It was, I think now, some sort of rite of passage. He was choosing to love a woman so much...older. My hair was long now, almost to my shoulders. I liked that it had a dark auburn shade. I knew when it fell forward, it hid my face.

As I bent down to put the spurs on, he leaned toward me at the same time. I kissed him, closing my eyes, inhaling his aftershave lotion.

He kissed back.

His lips were warm and tender. We stood, kissing, wrapped our arms around one another. How good it was to be touched after so long.

Then.

We walked into the living room. Arms linked at our waists, to the couch.

He pulled me on top.

I felt the crotch of his jeans. *Yes.*

Then.

"You'd better go home now."

"Why?"

"Because I want you to. I'm not sure...I need time to think...so do you...please, Tommy."

He looked at me for long moment. Then, "Goodbye for now," he said and kissed me quickly on the lips.

He skipped down the front steps like Fred Astaire. At the bottom he turned. "I have to go out and make some money," he called, jogging back down the street.

Cossack Hats

My parents eloped to West Virginia on June 17, 1931, and for two years my father continued to live at home with seven of his unmarried brothers and sisters. When I was born on April 1 the following year, he had another secret to keep from his father, Max Azen. My mother Torie lived with her brother and sister in an attic apartment with wicker furniture across town. Meanwhile, I was with Mutah, in Charleroi, learning to play with rosary beads, blissful and unaware that I had any other family or that a drama was unfolding.

"You couldn't tell me yourself?" my grandfather Azen says. "I have to find out from Mr. Cohen? 'So,' he says, 'how's by you and your *schon* family? How about the boy what married the *shiksa*? I hear they have a beautiful little girl.'"

"I knew you'd be upset, Papa," my father says.

"Upset? Upset? Who's upset? If I had a son who marries a *shiksa* I would be upset. I don't have such a son."

Max insists that the rest of the family join him in mourning. They cover the mirrors, walk about in cloth slippers, wear clothing with a rip in the lapel—that age-old expression of grief, symbolic of the pain caused by a heart ripped out of its chest.

By the time I'm ten, my father has managed to rise from the dead, so to speak, and I'm a regular visitor at Max Azen's Furs on Wood

Street in Pittsburgh. First floor: dresses and hats. Second floor: furs. Third floor: cloth coats. In Russia my grandfather had made hats for the Cossacks and resided above his furrier shop in Davinsk. He made a good living, so there was plenty of money for a hotel room when he traveled to Kiev to sell his furs, but he had to sleep on a straw mat in the train station because he was a Jew. Cossacks didn't welcome Jews into their military elite, but the Russian army wasn't fussy, conscripting boys like his sons for its wars. Why should he sacrifice them to fight for a country that wouldn't give him a room for the night?

In 1901 Max booked passage for Boston, America, then a train for Pittsburgh where Mr. Jacobson, Bessie and Max's brother-in-law, met the family at the station with his wagon and took them in. The rags-to-riches story brings us to forty years later when my grandfather is supplying Pittsburgh with fur coats, jackets, and stoles—mink or sable to elite patrons, raccoon or Persian lamb for the middle-class wives, rabbit and pony coats for the less fortunate—and I'm spending afternoons with the women who pieced the furs together and altered clothing on the two uppermost floors of Max's establishment. The seamstresses made a fuss over me, keeping me entertained, sometimes spilling a box of straight pins on the table where they assembled coats, giving me a giant magnet to pick them up.

I loved to play with the furs, especially sheared beaver and leopard. No one thought it was wicked to kill animals for ornament then. I would lie on the skins, rub my face on them. They were lifeless, yes, but they smelled warm to me, their odor unique and irresistible, a kind of life after death.

Mazel

As THE STORY GOES, MY mother and father were enjoying a rare evening dining out when all was forgiven. My father had taken to selling life insurance when he was no longer welcome working for Max Azen Furs, and he was flush with a twenty-dollar commission that night. He joked that my mother had ordered the most expensive entrée on the menu: chicken ala king.

Through an ingenious method, my father had just that morning caught the thief stealing milk bottles from the threshold of their basement apartment on Munhall Road. As I imagine it, he lies sleeping on his back next to Torie, my mother, in the Murphy bed, his arms behind his head. He waits, listening, staring into the dark.

He wiggles his foot to test the strength of the thread twined around his big toe. It'll hold, he tells himself. The thread trails along the bed to the carpet, across the living room, and under the door. The other end is tied to the glass milk bottle, just delivered, in the hall; the cream is rising to the top.

He strikes a match in order to see the face of Little Ben—the morning is crawling into its fifth hour. He strikes a second match and lights a Camel, lies in bed smoking, appreciating the fierce red glow from the burning cigarette in the darkness. He stubs out the cigarette.

Nothing. A panel of gray creeps across the high barred window just above street level. The clock clucks. His wife breathes, in, out. He slides into a doze, comes awake, drifts off to sleep again.

Then a tug on his toe, and he is awake, at the door, yanking it open. "Got you, you bastard!" He grabs the stranger bent over the milk.

They wrestle, the bottle slips from the thief's hand. Glass splinters, milk splatters on the tile. My father loses his grip, and the man wrenches free, runs up the steps and out the entryway. All he's seen are black pupils filled with fear, or hope, he can't tell, a few missing teeth, a shabby brown coat, a cap pulled low. Maybe he smelled a whiff of garlic.

Then comes the windfall and the dinner at Conte's.

"Table for two," my father says, escorting my mother behind the maître d'.

They study the menu. He orders two Brandy Alexanders. They wait for their dinners.

Around them sit fat ladies in fur coats, probably his father's furs. The busboy fills their water glasses. My father looks up as the man scuttles off, says, "That guy looks familiar."

"You never forget a face," my mother says.

More time passes. Their food comes. The busboy returns with more water.

Now we're in a scene Rod Serling could have written for *The Twilight Zone*:

"You're the guy I caught I this morning! Stealing milk! On Munhall Road!" my father says.

"Please, mister. The boss is giving me such a look."

"Sit down. Tell me the truth."

"I'll lose my job. Okay, maybe tell the boss you're my cousin."

"He'll believe that?"

The thief sits. My mother passes the rolls.

"I just got the job this morning and how much you think a *shlepper* like me makes?"

My mother is fidgeting by now. "Don't be hard on him. Give him some money. Give him ten. How many children do you have, Mr. Busboy?"

"Some people got *mazel*. Some don't. I'd take a little fruit, too, if you don't mind."

"Give him the money," my mother says.

My father reaches in his pocket, hands over the bill. "Just don't come back or I'll beat the crap out of you."

"That's no way to give a gift," my mother adds. "Say something nice."

"What kind of *schlemiel* do you think I am?" my father says.

The busboy hears an exit cue and takes it, wiping his forehead on a napkin as he makes for the kitchen.

The band is playing "My Blue Heaven." A slight but dignified bald man with a cane, wearing spats and a pearl-gray vest and jacket, walks over to their table.

"Love, love, with twelve children I should understand love, but still, what do I know?"

My father's eyes open wide like a horse before a race. "What are you doing here?"

"So, *nu*, introduce me already." The man nods his head, smiles at my mother behind his stiff white mustache.

"You know my husband?"

"Know him? I shouldn't know him? I know him already for twenty-six years. It's you I don't know."

"Torie. I'm glad to meet you."

"Papa, I…"

"It's time I meet this wife of yours. And the baby. I see what you do," Max Azen continues. His eyes are hazy with remembering. "You know, in the Jewish religion *tzedaka* is what's important. To live righteously, to help others. Welcome to the family, Torie Azen."

You Think That's Bad: Three

‿‿

WHEN I FINALLY DECIDED TO leave Jack, my best friends Marian and Helen came over to show me they "were there for me." They sat in the darkened family room, which in those days was called the rec room, to "commiserate." They hadn't known what I'd been going through. I'd told no one. Not my best friends, not even Steffie.

"How could you not tell me?" she'd said. "I thought you had the perfect marriage! I felt *guilty* because you seemed to have such a great sex life. Zola wanted to have it every night, and I said no. You never said no."

Maybe I didn't trust anyone enough to talk about the pain. Maybe I thought I could fix things.

Years before, Marian and I had been the ones sitting in Helen's rec room waiting for her illegal abortion to work. That day it was the same dim light, the same depression, only with talking.

All I wanted to do was clean out the drawers built into the wall at the end of the room. I kept my back to them. Finally they left. I was glad.

A Liberated Woman

Yes, it's true.

After the divorce I moved into an old mansion that had been subdivided into apartments. The two-bedroom apartment was ugly but had a turret with a window seat and a fireplace—the two amenities that convinced me to rent it for Lauren and me.

One night I lay on the carpet in front of the fire—my daughter was on a date—and indulged myself in a review of the traumatic last few months. I had heard somewhere that women were burning their bras, and now seemed as good a time as any for a symbolic gesture of liberation.

I unbuttoned my blouse and tossed my beige nylon bra into the flames where it sort of melted and disintegrated. A perfectly good twenty-dollar piece of underwear, gone.

It wasn't as thrilling as I'd hoped.

Got the Get

TOMMY, LAUREN, AND I WERE in Los Angeles for the baseball season. I had no idea why I wanted a *get*, the legal document executed by a rabbi or Jewish court of law that would dissolve my marriage to Jack. I had no plans to remarry Tommy or anyone else. What I seemed to need, though, was a definitive end to my first life so that I could go on living my second one—if there was going to be one.

We drove up the steep mountain to the University of Judaism. Tommy and Lauren waited in the car.

I didn't know the three rabbis who chanted the ancient prayers in Hebrew, but they were kind and sympathetic; it was nothing like the ordeal of the legal divorce in Pittsburgh at which a fat attorney with a booming voice had stood asking me questions.

The rabbi's words, delivered with gentle intonation, washed over me, and I couldn't stop crying. I felt sorrow, but also, perhaps relief. One of them patted me on the shoulder for comfort.

And then it was over.

Signpost up Ahead

Here is what I knew:

I had divorced my husband of twenty-three years.

My children had left home except Lauren.

I wanted to leave Pittsburgh and live in a small town.

I loved the outdoors, loved horses and dogs and skiing.

I ran across an article about the actor Robert Redford who had built a resort in Sundance, Utah. (I decided to forgive him for starring with Barbra Streisand in *The Way We Were*.) The dream of a cabin of my own on the top of a mountain materialized.

I was forty-six years old. A man who was eighteen years younger said he was in love with me, said, *Let's go*.

I sold the house, put my furniture in storage. Packed the Jeep and drove west with Lauren, Tommy, and the cat.

I thought: *my grandparents on both sides left Russia and Germany, respectively, knowing they could never go back. But I can always go back to Pittsburgh.*

It took us four days to the reach the signpost that pointed east to PARK CITY and west to SALT LAKE CITY.

"Which way?" Tommy asked.

It was a glorious day in October 1978. All over town in Park City were construction workers without shirts, sawing, hammering, atop ladders, calling to one another, playing loud music on radios. We found a condo for rent, cheap, because it was off-season in this place waiting for the snows to blanket the ski runs. Off-season: that seemed right. I was waiting, too—but for what, I wasn't sure.

Part Two
The Majors

Southland: One

1986. Leaning my head against the window, I could feel the chill of the March morning in the glass. A cold front had moved in.

We'd awakened at five thirty in the dark to drive to Shelbyville, Tennessee, for an eleven-thirty appointment with a player and his family. Brian was a boy Tommy had picked from his study of stats over the winter.

The town's main street was verdant, homey. We pulled into the parking lot in front of the family's grocery store. Both grandparents still worked there alongside Brian's father and his mother, Betty. Brian, a pitcher starting his second year in A-ball was going to spring training in Florida the next day.

Tommy brought Brian's father out to meet me: a thin pleasant-looking man in a short-sleeved shirt and grocer's apron. I shook his hand through the window.

Brian pulled up in his new black Honda, grinning—a goofy smile. His face was heavy, pink; his crew-cut hair was the texture and hue of hay. He led us to his house.

"Come in, come in," Betty said, in a soft drawl, waving us through the door into the living room. A pool table, a big TV, mounts: a buck and a doe staring back with blank resignation, thanks to the taxidermist's work. Trophies lined built-in shelving, from ceiling to floor, the entire length and width of the room. An exercise bike. Weights and dumbbells around it.

"You must be thirsty after your long drive," Betty said. She was a tall, handsome woman. I noticed her evaluating me as most mothers did before she headed to the kitchen. She returned with the tray of beverages and little cucumber sandwiches and cookies.

On the lower shelf of the coffee table was a great black book, embossed with THE HOLY BIBLE. Above the mantle hung a portrait of the family outdoors, sitting on a log, framed by autumn foliage.

"I always have a portrait done outdoors since we like to be outside so much," Betty said. She was pleased I'd noticed. But for me, a pang, too: I'd wanted what she seemed to have, stability, consistency, season after season. And I sensed something else: this was a woman who took her job seriously, to protect her daughter, her son, and her husband from predators—such as baseball agents.

Brian turned out to be a talker, a whiner, going on about being cheated, not given a fair chance, not appreciated for what he could do.

"All I got paid last year was nine hundred a month and this year, a thousand. That doesn't even cover my car payments and gas and insurance.

"But that's all anyone makes in Single-A ball," Tommy said.

"Yeah, but they're cheating all of us. The other guys are making millions."

"In the big leagues." Tommy looked him in the eyes, didn't blink.

"Exactly. If I were in the big leagues, I'd make some real money."

"Your job now is to pitch the very best you can, get moved up to Double-A next year and on up, Brian. You'll do fine."

"Yeah, but right now they're really cheating me."

Tommy and I exchanged looks. Another spoiled kid from Little League through college who was used to being a star.

Brian's dad walked in then and sat next to Tommy.

"We get up most mornings at five during the summer to throw the ball around," he said. "I love the game, and I always wanted my boy to love it too."

"They barely eat dinner so they can get outside at the end of the day to play some more before it gets dark," Betty added. "I surely don't know why I even bother to cook." She smiled at Brian and his dad.

Beyond the window was a lovely lake spanning a flat, grassy meadow, reflecting sunlight rippling across the high ceiling. A dog barked from the woods beyond. Betty said the lake was filled with fish and frogs and giant turtles.

"One bit off a duck's leg. The frogs croak all night until sometimes the neighbors complain, but I don't know what we can do about it. The property stretches all the way to that line of loblolly pines."

"What are those little yellow flowers in the grass that look like daffodils?" I said.

"Buttercups. They grow thicker and thicker every year."

Brian's sister came in and sat next to her mother. Tall, slender, probably a good athlete, too. We were being interviewed, it seemed, by the whole clan.

Next: the scrapbooks of photos and clippings, Brian as a baby, Brian in Little League, Brian playing football in high school.

"How did you decide to give up football for baseball?" Tommy said.

"I thought I could play both, but then knew I had to make a choice. I always knew I wanted to play baseball."

Brian's dad shared a clipping of his son pitching a shut-out and getting the MVP award in high school for the entire central Tennessee district. He'd once played ball himself, he said, but was nowhere as good as Brian.

"Grandpa'll be having a fit if I don't get back to store soon," he said.

The television droned in the background. Five hours had passed, but by then Brian was referring to Tommy as "my agent."

Betty mentioned that she and her girlfriends walked five miles every day in a little park just down the road. "In the summer we get up at five in the morning before the temperature gets too high. Even if it's eighty degrees."

"If you wouldn't mind, I'd love to go over there before it gets too late," I said.

Betty stood up immediately. "I'll drive you and come back for you after."

"I got to go take some animals to the taxidermist in the next town before I leave tomorrow," Brian said. "Come on with me, Tommy. Mom, you'll have to pick them up for me in a few days."

Tommy would tell me later about driving with Brian, the dead animals tucked in the trunk of the car on newspapers, their mouths agape in death.

I'd tell him about my jog in the woods. How Betty would meet me after my tenth lap, introduce me to an older couple as Brian's agent's wife, and then share all her thoughts on blacks and their knowing "their place."

Brian signed before we left that day and we celebrated. But on the way out of town I looked out the window ahead at the row of dotted lines like stitches sewn down the middle of the highway.

"Maybe someday when we make it," I said, "We'll be allowed to say what we're really thinking."

Moss and Oak

THE DREAM DISSOLVED, DEMATERIALIZED: I had been in a room, fully furnished, populated with guests, then the door slammed shut...and someone was pounding on it.

"Open up in there. Police!"

I pulled the curtain aside. There was a cruiser, its turret lights flashing, red, white, and blue. It was long past midnight.

I shook Tommy awake. "Just a minute," he yelled, pulling on his trousers, opening the van door. "What's the problem?"

"What are you doing here?" She was a sturdy, muscular woman, hands big as a man's, a flashlight in one and a billet club in the other.

"Step out, please. Who's with you?"

"My wife. We've been traveling late, officer, and just pulled up here beside the lake. It looked like such a nice quiet spot. I'm an agent for baseball players..."

I wasn't his wife, but under the circumstances, an economy of communication was probably best. She flashed the light around the interior of the van, catching me still under the bedclothes.

"You'll have to leave."

"The cat, Tommy, tell her about the cat."

We let Lady out at night to roam—a worrisome adaptation at first to our months on the road. But it seemed so unfair to keep her constantly imprisoned. After so many months, we'd become a little complacent: she always came back.

"Registration and driver's license, please."

"We didn't realize we were doing anything wrong…"

"This here's private property. And a construction site. You could've been stealing equipment or something. You can stay until morning. Just be sure you're gone by seven before the workmen get here. Goodnight."

"That was scary."

"Scary?" Tommy said. "That scared the crap out of me. I thought we were being robbed."

At first light, we started calling for Lady. Tommy whistled and banged a spoon against her cat bowl. I propped open the van door and ran the electric can opener—which I thought was ingenious. Still no Lady. I could smell the murky odor of plant sludge and mud. How would we find her in the middle of nowhere? Tommy had appointments to keep.

"I told you we shouldn't bring her on these trips," I said.

"What were we going do, put her in a kennel for five weeks? She'd never survive."

"I might not survive this," I said.

A magpie landed nearby, curious about the commotion or eager for a handout. Then, at the far edge of the lake, as the morning sun edged above the tree-line, out pranced Lady Samantha.

Once we were underway, she tucked herself in next to Tommy as usual for a nap, her front paws and head draped across his leg. He stroked her as he drove.

Tennessee. South Carolina. Georgia. On Sundays the radio stations of the deep South broadcast ministers preaching hellfire and brimstone, or others, such as one female pastor, tried offering messages of hope: *O wrestlin' Jacob. Jacob day's a-breakin. I will not let thee go! O wrestlin' Jacob. Jacob's day's a-comin'. He will not let me go!*

One program, "The Obituaries of the Air," commenced with somber funeral music, which faded in and out as a woman with a heavy southern accent began reading: "Lula Mae McDowell Speed, aged forty-eight, died in Holy Cross Hospital yesterday after a long illness, attended by her family. Lula's husband and two children and her three sisters were among the bereaved. Services and the viewing have been scheduled for..."

My mother had recently died, and my father, two years before her. I was thinking of them the day we camped at a KOA in Alabama by a gray lake.

The morning dawned overcast and cool, a thick fog lingering over the water. Fishermen were already strung along the shore casting. *Hiss, plop. Hiss, plop.* Several boats were trolling with lines trailing.

We walked the campground's dirt roads, Tommy and I, beneath old-growth live oaks, dripping with Spanish moss. A forest fire had scorched underbrush in places and blackened trees, but beneath them, green shoots had sprung up.

A river cut a wide swath, pouring itself into the lake. We came upon what was left of a duck, limp body intact but headless.

"Think a dog got it?"

"Lady isn't much bigger than that. She's so vulnerable."

"I'd feel vulnerable without you," Tommy said, taking me into his arms.

Wash Day

AT NOON TOMMY DROPPED ME off at a laundromat in the tiny town of Cowarts, population two hundred. The floor was filthy: lint clumps; emptied, soggy boxes of detergent; candy wrappers. Machines sat atilt. The folding table was worn, rickety. He couldn't leave me here for three and a half hours while he made his next appointment. Couldn't.

I hurried after him to the grocery store appended to the laundromat where he'd gone to buy soap. The stench inside was overwhelming: something dead, decaying. A rat or maybe a stray cat without a litter box. We wandered the aisles until we found a broken-down shelf and a few battered boxes of detergent.

"Get out of here, now, before I whup you black asses. You hear? I ain't puttin' up with you." The man was white, wearing a yellow nylon shirt with buttons that strained to span his big belly. The girls scampered ahead of him like puppies, feet bare, bony long legs.

"Why would you talk to two little children like that?" Tommy said. His tone was modulated, careful.

"Damn little niggers. Come in here for candy and don't have no money."

Tommy handed over ten dollars for the soap, asking for change in quarters.

"That's what we call 'em around here, *niggers*."

Tommy grabbed the detergent then, ripped open the box and poured it on the floor. "We don't need your soap, but you need to clean up your act."

"And *nigger* once meant lazy worker, which seems to be what you are," I said.

Silence.

"You can get out of my store, too," the man growled.

A Bar in Homewood

As I've said, I consider it a dubious talent, this ability to fit in, to put people at ease, the reason being is that it stems from acute insecurity, from needing to prove that I'm worthy.

Jack and his friend Joe nicknamed the bar that Jack bought "The Office" so that if your wife asked you where you'd been when you got home late, you could answer truthfully. Only none of the men who hung out at the bar worked in an office—they were blue-collar steel workers from this tough Pittsburgh neighborhood. All white. Two weeks after ownership changed hands, it became an all-black bar overnight, and Joe, who ran the place, was scared enough to quit. The next bartender was black. I baked pies and went to The Office with Jack once a week to deliver them. I danced with the patrons. I even ate chitlins—the worst thing I'd ever tasted—and proclaimed them delicious.

In short I won them over. But that isn't much of an achievement, is it, if you have no idea who you are really, what your authentic self is like, and whether, if you did, anyone would actually like you for yourself.

Southland: Two

1986. Another town in Tennessee.

Another family meeting in another home.

"What do you think my chances are for making it into the big leagues?" Jerry asked. He reached for a tiny round piece of the white bread topped with a slice of cheese.

"If you work hard and are patient, there's no telling how far you'll go," Tommy said.

"Yes, but what are the chances? The statistics," Jerry's mom said.

"Baseball is easier than football," Tommy explained. "In football, twenty thousand boys play at the college level. Only four hundred, or two percent, are drafted, and only one percent go to the NFL. College *is* their minor league."

"Right now, only four percent of the boys in the minor leagues ever get called up to the majors for even a cup of coffee," Jerry said.

"A cup of coffee?"

"That's an expression, Mom, for boys that go up to the big league for a day or two and are sent right down. Trouble today is there's so many boys from Puerto Rico and the Dominican. They can get those boys for a thousand bucks and a uniform. They take up all the places on the roster."

"A lot of players from other countries are getting into the game," Tommy said.

"They don't even speak English."

"They learn pretty fast."

"Do you know why some people call Latinos *spicks*?" I said. "I just read it the other day in the dictionary. It's because they didn't *spic* such good English."

"Really," Ellen said.

"And *wop* stood for immigrants without papers. The word *kike* came from Ellis Island in the late 1800s. The officer would ask an immigrant Jewish person to sign his or her name and when they said they were illiterate, he told them to make an x. That they would never do, make the sign of the cross, so in exasperation, the officer told them to just make a circle. The Yiddish word for circle is *kikel*."

"I hope you don't mind my asking, are you of the Jewish persuasion?" Ellen said.

"Why, yes, we are," Tommy said. "I hope that doesn't make any difference."

"Of course not. I was just curious, and I know that some of the smartest people in the world are Jews."

"We've put a lot of emphasis on studying and learning over the years."

"That certainly must account for the success of your people in so many fields."

"What kind of a percentage do you take?" Jerry asked.

"I don't charge anything until you make it to the big leagues and are earning $109,000. After that it's four percent of the whole amount."

"I've heard that literary agents and those in show business make between ten and fifteen percent," said Ellen.

"That would certainly be nice, but we don't charge anything near that."

I had heard all this before; I gazed around the room. Floor-to-ceiling doors that opened onto a deck with a view of a gently sloping landscape of trees, blue sky, and masses of spring flowers bursting into bloom. Inside, the walls were covered with framed photographs and newspaper articles. A handsome man in a football uniform was the star of the family assemblage.

"That's my husband," Ellen said. He was a great football player in his day." She sighed. "Jerry has his heart set on baseball. He always has, but if it doesn't work out, he'll come back and finish college."

"I'm going to make it, Mother. When do I sign the contract?"

"Not until you and your family are ready," Tommy said. "I ask my boys to just give me chance to show what I can do, and then they can sign when they feel sure. All I'm asking is that you don't sign with anyone else, give me the opportunity to be your agent, and then later on we'll do the paperwork."

"I certainly feel better about that," Ellen said. "The last thing my husband said as he went off to work this morning was not to let Jerry sign anything. Naturally I accept his word, but knowing you aren't in a rush makes me feel better too."

"Dad's been in professional sports and is kind of careful of contracts," Jerry said.

"Brad's a lawyer with an old firm that his father founded. He was such a hero in his day people still like to come in just to talk to him. He's the kind of man who knows what he wants and can't be pushed into anything, and he doesn't want his family pushed either, no matter how competent the person seems." Ellen sighed again.

"There's all the time in the world. You'll see what a good job I can do, and then you'll be sure," Tommy said.

"Come on outside and let me show you my batting cage," Jerry said. "Mind if we leave you ladies for a while?"

The wind blew through the pines. Shadows danced on the hardwood floors.

I followed Ellen through a tour of her lovely home. I heard about her and her husband's lives together: high-school sweethearts. Never another man for her.

"Well, of course my husband would have liked Jerry to be a football player, but I'm much happier. I don't think his chances of getting hurt are as great. Baseball seems like a gentler sport."

"I know prominent doctors and businessmen who would give their eyeteeth to be a professional player. Every man wants to play ball. I read some place that the saddest day of a man's life is when he realizes he's finally too old to be a professional player."

"Can you imagine?" Ellen said. "A woman would never feel that way about a game. She would spend her energies seeing that her family succeeds and gets what it should in this world, but dedicate herself to baseball? Never."

"Some women have dedicated their lives to sports, actually. Tennis, golf. Female Olympians." I smiled.

"Yeh-uss, I think it's marvelous for women to play tennis and golf, but only for fun, for social reasons, never for a living. Those women are all lesbians."

"Some women do pick alternative lifestyles."

"If my daughter Sally turned out to be a lesbian, I'd kill myself. That's what I'd do, just shoot myself or take pills or something. I couldn't live with it. Do you have children, Joanne?"

"Three by a former marriage, all grown now."

"If you don't mind my asking, how long were you married to your first husband?"

"Twenty-three years."

"That *is* a long time. You stayed until the children grew up."

"Not really. That would be taking credit for something that isn't true. My first husband was quite a womanizer. I left when I realized that no matter how hard I tried, things would never change."

"Where are my manners? I'm asking too many personal questions. I apologize."

Back in the living room after the tour, we strolled out onto the deck.

"How old are you and Tommy, if you don't mind me asking?"

"You see, I'm quite a bit older than he is," I said with a practiced smile.

"Oh, really."

Jerry called to us; he and Tommy were below in the driveway. "What are you two ladies gabbing away about?"

"Nothing, just woman talk," Ellen said, laughing.

The Movie of Our Lives: One

WE ALMOST MADE ONE A couple of decades ago. A friend of Tommy's, Al, liked the story and thought he had the right connections in Hollywood. So, what actors did we want to play us? For me, Tommy voted Sharon Stone; I thought Susan Sarandon would be a better pick. An actress of her caliber could pull off the woman I once was: self-confident on the outside—the right clothes, the right make-up— who's an insecure mess underneath them.

For his mother's character, Tommy said he'd cast Doris Roberts from the sitcom *Everybody Loves Raymond*—or Roseann Barr. Bossy, brash—*irritating,* in a word.

"J Lo," his mother voted, "and Richard Gere for Poppy."

What Al had in mind was a comical farce, say, with scenes such as Scott Boras chasing Tommy around the bases at a ballpark. Suffice it to say, Al just didn't *get it.*

An Incident at Little Dell

I HADN'T BEEN THINKING COHERENTLY when I'd packed for the move. I mailed all my heavy books instead of storing them and instead stored sheets, blankets, and pillows that we would need as soon as we got to Utah. Together Tommy and I bought a big cardboard box and lugged the TV to the Greyhound Bus Station and shipped it to General Delivery since it was too big for the post office to take. Every day, Tommy, swearing and angry; every day, me, insisting that my things were important and his were junk. Every day there were more boxes for Tommy to mail. Ninety-nine boxes of stuff on the way. The postage eventually amounted to a thousand dollars. That's how stupid I could be. I'd been counting on a man to be in charge my entire life—my father, then Jack—but this time I was with a mere boy.

Having arrived in Park City, we started house-hunting. Real estate agents showed little interest in finding a rental property for us in town, so we scouted outlying communities: Heber, Midway, Kamas, and a little speck called Samak—Kamas spelled backwards. When told that a place had "no winter access," we said, "That's okay," because city-folk like us had no idea what that meant. A condo in Park City became available for $500 a month: two bedrooms, a loft, and a Jacuzzi bathtub. The owners' son had recently died in an automobile accident, and they didn't plan on using that second dwelling any time soon.

I was squeamish about taking advantage of another's tragedy but, walking through the bright, airy rooms, we knew we'd found a home. Two weeks later we moved in, sort of. My furniture wouldn't come for almost a month—the TV *had* been delivered, but that was it. The three of us, Tommy, Lauren, and I unrolled our sleeping bags on the living room floor.

Getting Lauren back into treatment was a priority, so we drove to Salt Lake City to meet with a psychiatrist whom her doctor in Pittsburgh had recommended, Paul Wender, author of *Mind, Mood, and Medicine.*

"What drugs have you taken?" he asked Lauren, leaning across his desk. He was a short, nervous man with white hair, bushy eyebrows, and intensely direct eyes.

"Marijuana, cocaine, LSD, speed," she told him. I detected a sense of pride.

"Angel dust?" He seemed relieved when Lauren said no, explaining that it did irreparable damage to the teenagers who used it.

We were extremely surprised when he said Lauren was still quite psychotic. I accepted his conclusion that Lauren belonged in a day-treatment center, assuming that I was so accustomed to her behavior I'd missed some cues. Her current medications were approved, and he assured us the center would refill them each week.

But how were we going to get Lauren to Salt Lake, some thirty miles from Park City, every day? No public transportation existed. A woman responded to my ad in the *Park Record* for a carpool, and arrangements were set for Lauren to be at the center Mondays and Fridays.

One day at the beginning of February, a particularly bitter winter day, the carpool was cancelled. Lauren was supposed to be at the treatment center by nine o'clock, and since Tommy was teaching as a substitute that day, it was up to me to transport her.

Thick cottony streamers of clouds wound around the mountain summits. The Jeep was iced up. Lauren and I lost time scraping the windshield and warming the engine. I did my best to swallow my apprehension about driving Parley's Canyon to the valley, telling myself, with a stoicism I learned from the nuns back in high school, to take each problem as it came.

Lauren sat beside me fiddling with the radio to find a station she liked. The music blared, but I knew it helped drown out the voices she still heard on occasion.

"Mother," she said, "you don't know what it's like to be inside my head. I wish we could have brain transplants and trade brains for an hour so that you'd understand what schizophrenia's like, and I could see what it's like to be normal for a while."

"I'd do that in a minute if it would help," I said. "At least it's winter, and you don't have to hear crickets anymore."

"That was awful."

"Put on your seat belt."

We had less than forty minutes to get to the center. I wanted to drive confidently, like Tommy—only less aggressively. I kept pace with a big white vehicle in front me, and before I knew it, the speedometer read sixty-five.

"I'm not doing so badly," I said.

"You're doing fine! You're a good driver, Mother."

Ahead I saw a deer splayed on the road. Blood was smeared on the pavement. Its vacant eyes seemed to stare at us as we passed. Its exposed organs glistened, ruddy and still.

"I'm afraid of everything," Lauren said. "What would I do without you? I'm twenty and still need my mother."

"A time will come when you won't need me as much."

"When will that be?"

A tractor trailer passed me in the right lane, spraying slush on my windshield. I flinched. Patches of snow coated the pavement. Forty inches had fallen a few days before. In Pittsburgh, one inch of water equaled ten inches of snow. In the high-desert climate of Utah the ratio was one to thirty.

For the first time I noticed the shoes Lauren was wearing. High heels.

"You'll never be able to walk in those." The center had a field trip scheduled.

"Don't worry. I'll be fine."

"It doesn't make any sense."

"These are the shoes I want to wear, Mother. I want to wear these."

"And can you stop changing stations?"

"I didn't like that song."

"It makes me nervous."

"I won't listen to anything then." She started to snap the radio off.

"No, I didn't mean you had to do that." I started to say something else, but glanced out the window at Little Dell Reservoir on our right, noticed how bleak it looked now, the water a sullen gray, not the blue I remembered from the fall.

Then I felt the tires lose traction. We were airborne—*Mother! We're going to die!*—then rolling, hood over bumper.

The Jeep came to rest on its roll bar, the roof stripped away, the windshield, too. We were hanging upside down by our seatbelts. The radio was playing something sweet and slow.

"I told you not to wear those shoes."

"Stop treating me like a baby. I don't need your help *all* the time. Help yourself. Take some driving lessons."

All at once we were laughing.

That November When We All Lost It: Entry #1

NOVEMBER 6, 1991. WEDNESDAY 11:37 A.M.

SINCE LAST FRIDAY I HAVEN'T accomplished very much. My life has been in turmoil. Maybe it will help if I just write it all down. No self-editing, not this time.

I had called Lauren in the morning around ten thirty or so because I hadn't heard from her but figured she was at the Halloween dance at the center. She lived in Provo on her own now. When she answered the phone she was crying, which is not unusual.

"I've just had a hard day and a hard night. I had a terrible time at the dance. I don't want to talk about it now. Al is here."

"Okay," I said. "I'll talk to you tomorrow."

"Are you mad?"

"No, of course not. If you don't feel like talking, that's fine."

We hung up, and I didn't give it much thought. She has a lot of "bad" days. Someone looks at her funny or Tim does this or does that. I was glad that Al, a friend from a nice Mormon family, was there and I didn't have to listen to it. I'm so sick of hearing about Tim I could scream.

On Saturday morning, November 2, I got up at the usual time and started reading the Torah portion about the death of Sarah. Lauren's Hebrew name is Sarah. I hadn't finished it all when Leslie called, and we decided to go to Salt Lake City as planned even though I had to be back in Park City by two thirty to get to the book sale in Heber where I had volunteered to work from three to five. We were going to Price Savers and Burlington Coat Factory so I could look for new towels, and Leslie could get her stuff.

She was coming at eleven thirty. I jumped out of bed, took a shower, and got dressed. Just before she arrived I decided I better call Lauren and tell her I was going out for the day and that I would call her when I got home. I didn't want her to worry.

"Hi," I said.

"This is Cheryl," the voice that sounded so much like Lauren said. "I guess you heard."

My heart dropped. "Heard what?

"Lauren overdosed last night."

"What!?"

"She called me and said she felt suicidal. She was upset about Tim."

I felt like white-hot lightning had struck.

"She called back a second time and said she took ten Atavan, six hundred milligrams. I told her to stop taking pills and asked if she wanted me to come over to sleep. Then she called a third time and said she took four more. I told her she shouldn't do that. I get dramatic, too, when things go wrong but not that bad."

"And?"

"She called a fourth time and said she took four more, eighteen Atavan altogether. I asked again if she wanted me to sleep at her house, and she said yes. I could come over, and she would probably be dead in the morning. I called Todd, and he said we should call the police.

We called the poison control center, and they said that much could be lethal. By the time we got to Lauren's apartment she was passed out on the floor. I called the police and then the paramedics came. When they took her out in the ambulance her eyes were rolling back in her head. I was really scared. I've never been in an emergency like that before."

My legs seemed to break, and I slid down on the floor with my back against the wall. "You did the right thing, Cheryl. If it wasn't for you, she might not be here now."

She told me Lauren was in Utah Valley Hospital and gave me the number. I couldn't believe Tommy was still on the phone talking baseball when Lauren had tried to commit suicide. Tommy said he thought I was talking to Lauren and that Cheryl had tried to commit suicide.

I didn't know what to do. Leslie said I probably wasn't going to Salt Lake then, but for some strange reason, I didn't want her to leave. I didn't want to change my plans. I wanted the day to go on as usual, as if nothing had happened.

I called the hospital and got put on hold, then passed on to one connection after another. First I was told, "We can't give any information since she's an adult."

"I'm her mother!" I screamed.

I was finally transferred to Lauren's unit. I asked the nurse, a woman named Roz, what I should do.

"Whatever you feel like doing."

"I haven't had any experience with suicide. I want to do what is best for Lauren so this will never happen again."

"What do you feel like doing? These kids who do drugs are all the same." She didn't care that Lauren suffered from schizophrenia; to her my daughter was just another druggie.

"I feel like slapping her silly." For some reason that I didn't understand my first reaction was anger, strong, blinding, irrational anger.

If I had been near Lauren I would have beaten the crap out of her. *Do what I feel like doing?*

"I'm asking for your help," I said.

"She needs cigarettes. You could bring cigarettes."

"Wouldn't that just be rewarding her behavior?"

"Well, you do what you feel like."

I asked to talk to Lauren.

"Why did you do this?"

"I don't know why." My daughter started to cry, then stopped herself and said if she lost control they wouldn't let her out of there.

She said she was sorry, but when I asked her if she was ever going to do it again, there was a long pause and then she said she wouldn't. It wasn't very convincing. I told her I wasn't coming down, and I wasn't bringing cigarettes. I could tell she felt badly, and I was glad. She was very submissive, whatever I said was okay. All the fight had gone out of her, and she was feeling terribly guilty for what she had done. I wanted to punish her. Meanwhile, Leslie had gone to the post office. When she came back, we went to Salt Lake. I think she understood why I still wanted to go, but I didn't. I was just so upset.

I didn't want to go to Provo to see Lauren. I didn't want to stay at home. I didn't know what I wanted. We talked all the way to the valley about Lauren and Leslie's husband's business partner, whom Leslie hates. It did me good to hear about someone else's problems. We went to Burlington Coat Factory. I had never been there. I bought new towels. I had realized how old and torn and beat up my brown and wine and beige towels were. They were twelve years old and bought with a hundred dollars that Jack had given me for a house gift when he visited in 1979, and they made me feel terribly guilty. I got beige and black towels this time. I walked around and browsed. I saw the high boots that Lauren wanted and the pea coat. I kept looking for Hannukah presents for her for some strange reason. We left there and went to Price Savers. I had never been there either. It wasn't as nice as the first place.

Leslie looked for some crayons for her nephew and nieces for Christmas. I waited in line. It was so crowded that we decided to leave. It was getting late. I tried to talk her into going to the book sale in Heber, but it was better I went alone. I could drive and think. I needed time to think.

Memento Mori

1979

I CALLED THE SCHOOL AND told them to get a substitute. I called the airport. I packed and, after a moment's hesitation, put my black dress with the high neck and long sleeves in the suitcase. When I changed planes in Denver, I called the hospital.

The nurse said, "I'm very sorry. Your father died thirty minutes ago."

I boarded the second plane and kept my face toward the window so the man next to me wouldn't see I was crying. The sun shone behind the billows of cumulus clouds. On a piece of scrap paper I wrote all the things I could remember about him as the plane droned eastward. I was tired. I noticed I had torn one of my nails off close to the quick. I played with it, tried to make it smooth; I didn't have an emery board. Once we landed I never cried again, not in front of anyone, not in front of my mother. She was wearing a wig, having gone as bald as the men in my father's family, owing to the chemotherapy.

His last words to her as they'd wheeled him into the I.C.U.: "If anything happens to me, be sure pay off my gin-rummy debts. I owe Joe $275 and Marv $150.

And who was this person in the casket? This man whose lips were pulled shut across his teeth. He must have been a mouth-breather. Candlelight flickered across his face. I touched his finger. It wasn't a human finger but a hard, cold thing, like a taper. Someone hugged me and then someone else. I didn't think I'd miss him much.

1978

I'd moved out west, two thousand miles from them both, taking the youngest child with me. She'd had the schizophrenic break by then. My father's way of dealing with mental illness was to tell her every time he saw her, "Now repeat after me: Every day in every way I'm getting better and better."

1974

Jack and I told my parents we were divorcing. I told them it was my idea. You'd have thought the floor had fallen out from under them.

"Why would you get divorced when you finally have some financial security?" said my father.

Not, *What has he done to make you unhappy?*

1964

Retirement came too early, and my father grew bored with his golf and gin-rummy games. They returned to Pittsburgh where he bought his sister's little lamp store. Hundreds of lamps and chandeliers, crystal and brass, all sizes and shapes, illuminated the place. Customers ducked the lights hanging from every inch of ceiling. When I'd worked there for him, he'd check every sales slip I wrote, every price tag I hung on a shade. Eavesdrop on and critique my every sales conversation. My father's name, Philip, meant "Giver of Light," the rabbi had said at the funeral.

He found he could work some and still play golf and gin rummy at the country club. The lamp business was run into the ground. My parents, living beyond their means, soon found they had no means.

1959

The night we all gathered around the Thanksgiving table, the pain that gripped his chest and down his left arm left us with mouths full of turkey.

At the hospital his doctor said, "He finally had the heart attack he'd been waiting for." But smoking and eating after golf continued to be his second and third favorite sports.

"No more women/no more furs/no more brothers' dirty words," he hummed as he left the family business and moved to Florida. He was fifty years old. I was twenty-seven.

I need to get to know him, I'd said to the wall.

1958

My father and mother attended obligatory dinners at our house every two weeks or so. He bought fifty-cent hamburgers from the White Tower for our dog and made Bozo jump and beg. My father insisted on carving the chicken or roast. He licked his fingers and smacked his lips and breathed through his nose like an old furnace when his mouth was full. My first husband was disgusted. My father's opinion of Jack was better kept to himself.

1957

Back in college, I got pregnant for the third time, but finished the bachelor's degree all the same. I waddled across the brightly lit stage, the black robe hiding the baby's bulge, and was handed my diploma. I looked across the footlights for his face. My father paid as much attention to graduation day as I did to the Super Bowl.

1954

I went to college until I had my second child.

1952

I went to college until I had my first child.

1951

I asked my father why he thought we were put on earth, if he believed God created us, if he agreed with Dostoevsky, if he understood infinity.

"Don't be silly. Smarter people than you have tried to figure these things out and couldn't. Just forget about them," he said.

I had betrayed him by growing up.

I broke up with my boyfriend and dated one from Ohio.

"He seems so unstable. We don't think he's the right one for you," they said.

I married the handsome, wealthy boy down the street.

"We don't approve of him. He's wild. He'll never make a good husband," they said.

Sometimes I watch the home movies of the wedding. My father looks as if he's escorting me to a funeral.

1950

I spent my evenings sitting up in bed knitting argyle socks and writing daily letters to my boyfriend in Philadelphia.

"We really don't like him. He's cheap," my father said. "That purse he gave you for Christmas looks like he got it at a garage sale. We want a man that's taller (shorter, fatter, thinner) for you."

Our first TV set: mostly there was dead time with nothing on but the test pattern. Then came the night of the Joe Louis fight against Ezra Charles for the heavyweight championship. My father invited his friend over to watch.

"Kill that nigger!" the friend screamed at the two black men on the screen.

"Don't use that word in our house," I said.

The friend didn't answer.

"Apologize," my father said.

"He really should," I said.

"No, I meant *you* apologize to *him*."

I went to my room, slammed the door, and sat at my desk. I waited and waited for my father to come and tell me I had done the right thing.

1949

I was a girl in blue jeans and old English boots, trotting my mare along the narrow, wooded path beside the stream. She stumbled and fell, crushing my knee beneath her. Then she tripped and fell more often. We called the vet.

"Periodic ophthalmia," he said.

Her dark eyes clouded over with blindness. My dad arranged for Mr. Schecter to take her for a brood mare. Her first foal would be mine someday.

We rode the hills up behind the stables for the last time. Once we'd galloped across the meadow, sure-footed, light-hearted. I patted her neck and murmured goodbye. I dismounted, drew her head against me, and buried my face in her neck, tears wetting her flaxen mane.

"How can I let him take you away?"

Mr. Schecter loaded her into the horse trailer. I watched it rattle down the lane, then wandered into the empty stall and slumped down on the straw. The sun poured through the top half of the Dutch door turning the straw to the color of her coat. After a while I walked home.

My father sat at the kitchen table in his undershirt reading the sports page, eating a bowl of Rice Krispies.

"Linen Lass is gone," I said.

He took another spoonful of cereal and wiped his mouth. "Don't think this means you can go away to school."

1947

The deal was, if my parents bought me a horse, I had to go to college right here in town and live at home. I fell in love with a palomino, Spanish for "resembling a dove."

1946

We'd come to Canada, Silver Birch Island at Lake Timagami, to fish in July. Out on the icy lakes in the later afternoon, my father couldn't get the outboard motor started. The sun cast a funnel of light across the waters; evergreens crowded the shores.

"I'll row us in," I said.

My mother fished with one hand and held a *Reader's Digest* in the other.

"I'll get it started. You don't have to row."

"I want to."

"Don't be silly. You can't row that far."

I rowed fast and hard, and he pulled on the starter cord, swearing under his breath. When I reached the dock my hands were blistered and bloodied. I hurried back to the cabin before he saw.

1945

After he left for the war my mother drank a lot. I went to the Catholic school far across town, too far to spend time with friends after classes. But I had horses for friends, and Milt to teach me to ride.

My father came back from Germany that summer after the war ended in Europe. I was in Bemus Point at the lake with my aunt and uncle and cousins, lying in the sun, swimming, walking on the sand. He drove up the day after he got home. I waited outside wearing my new dusty pink shorts with a matching shirt and a silk flower in my hair. He was wearing his uniform; his army cap snug on his bald head. He had lost a lot of weight.

My mother kept drinking. My father kept failing at his father's fur store. I kept riding horses.

1944

They would never draft him. That's what he said, anyway. He had influence in Washington and carried a briefcase of important papers everywhere.

That spring my mother and I followed him to army camps in Austin and El Paso, Texas. There were no apartments to rent so we lived in a hotel room downtown, and I went to a school called Rio Vista. In the gymnasium I danced with a handsome Latino boy, and the girls took me aside. "We don't dance with the spics."

I had to look it up: *spic n. Offensive. A Spanish-American person. [Perhaps from a mispronunciation of SPEAK.]*

One afternoon my mother and I saw my father marching with the other soldiers, but he was at the end of the line, panting through his mouth. The tall men were in front, the short ones in back. He was practically running to keep up. He advanced from private to technical sergeant fourth grade but was busted for gambling on the ship to England. He said they would never send him to Europe; he had influence.

We returned to Pittsburgh before he went overseas for good. Most of his family, ten of his eleven brothers and sisters and their spouses, crowded into our apartment to say goodbye. My mother was hysterical, sobbing, acting as if he were already dead. I was not going to cry, make a fool of myself like her.

"Be a good girl," he said and kissed me.

I kissed his cheek. "I will."

When he was gone, my mother screamed, "You didn't shed one tear, not one little tear for your poor father!"

Out the window the moon was sinking below the row of apartment buildings.

1943

Daddy sold our house. We moved to California where he was going to work in a defense factory and buy a ranch with my Uncle Sam, the doctor, so he wouldn't be drafted into the army. They took men with no children or only one child first.

Before we moved away, my parents had a surprise party for my eleventh birthday, April Fool's Day. I knew, but pretended I didn't. Donnie Yates came and all my friends. We played Spin the Bottle and Post Office in the laundry room. I wondered if I was doing it right. My mother and father were cooking hot dogs for us in the kitchen.

"This is the most fun I've ever had! We're playing kissing games!"

My father blanched and held his lips in a thin line. After that he was as distant as a train whistle in the night.

I cried all the way to California.

"Don't be silly," my father said.

His grandfather died suddenly before Memorial Day. When school let out, my mother and I and Mike the dog took the train back to Pittsburgh. My dad had rented an ugly apartment on the other side of town.

1942

My mother slept later and later in the mornings and took naps in the afternoons in her room with the door shut. In the evenings my father took her to the Bachelor's Club where he gambled—and where she learned to drink.

In November I went to the Ice Capades one afternoon with my friends. I didn't feel well. I had a strange sort of stomach ache. When I got home I laid down on the sofa and fell asleep. When I woke up, I went to the bathroom, finding a dark stain in my underpants. My mother said, "When your father comes home say, 'Today I am a woman.'" I felt stupid, but he congratulated me and made a tiny Brandy Alexander with crème de cacao and heavy cream for my cramps.

1941

I walked to Sunnyside School and Girl Scout meetings with a gaggle of girlfriends—and don't tell my folks—we'd ring-and-run at the neighbors' doors on the way. Under the streetlights at night we'd play Fox in the Morning and Red Rover. On summer evenings we'd catch fireflies after dinner, and in the spring we'd roam the woods, white with apple blossoms. Winters, we sledded and ice skated on a pond near the golf course.

My daddy said he loved animals, but he held our dog Mike's mouth closed, which made him mean. In our old house he'd hung our other dog on a coat hook for a minute or two to see his stupid expression.

"Daddy, don't do that," I said. "You'll hurt him."

"He doesn't mind."

My mother and I were changing the sheets one Sunday morning, December 7th, when we heard the news about a place called Pearl Harbor. That made me think about one night I was cuddling in bed with my daddy like I often did. I felt something hot and hard against my back. He got very upset and jumped out of bed and never cuddled with me again.

1940

My mother and I lived with my grandma while our house was being built. I worked in Mutah's garden with her among the cabbages and hollyhocks and sang songs from the Old Country. Two girls from my class stood on the hill above us: "Your mother smokes cig-ah-rettes. Your mother smokes cig-ah-rettes," they chanted.

In the middle of summer, we moved into our brand-new house. The electricity wasn't turned on yet, and I took a bath in a dark maroon tub lit by candles on the sink and the back of the toilet and around the edge of the tub. The flames threw shadows across the porcelain and everything smelled good, like new paint and fresh wood shavings. I was a princess.

The first New Year's Eve there my parents gave a party. Their voices and the music drifted up two flights of stairs. I sat up in bed reading *Little Women*. The wind howled around the corners of the house and ice pellets hit the windows. I leafed through the brand-new appointment book my daddy had given me with 1941 in gold letters on the front cover. Each day had its own page. I wrote my name and address on the first one.

I heard a soft knock on my door and my daddy came in to wish me happy New Year. He asked if I wanted the banana he'd brought.

I said, "Sure," happy because I wasn't allowed to eat before I went to sleep.

I reached for the banana and it was an empty skin, held together as if it still had the fruit in it. My daddy's eyes, nice dark-brown ones, squinched up laughing when he saw how surprised I was.

1939

Mother, Daddy, and I went to Conneaut Lake for the Labor Day weekend. We swam until the news came that Germany had attacked

Poland and started the war. My parents got very serious. I didn't know what war meant. I thought it was something exciting like in *Flash Gordon*.

My father was angry. "War is a terrible thing."

I stood in the shallow water and looked at my feet. Clouds passed over the sun. The sky turned dark.

That night they tucked me into bed and went downstairs in the hotel bar to talk. I read in *Life* magazine about the three kinds of mosquitoes and ate a Hershey bar very slowly. They took turns coming upstairs to check on me. I broke my candy bar into the tiny squares it came in and then each square into four pieces and made it last while I read and looked at the pictures of the bug.

1938

In first grade I learned a game called Monkey in the Corner. One night my mother and daddy and I played it. I said a verse and ran to the next corner before the other person got there. My daddy's pants fell down and I couldn't stop laughing. He had shorts underneath, big white boxer shorts that came down to his knees. He kept letting his pants fall down after that. I laughed so hard I fell on the floor. He put on his tap shoes and did a little dance. When he was young he and my Uncle Sam wanted to tap dance behind stage lights. He called it vaudeville.

My Uncle Sam became a doctor. He was bald like my daddy. My grandpa was bald too. My daddy worked in my grandpa's store selling fur coats. I liked to play in the fur skins, so soft, with a dried-meat smell mixed with moth balls.

The week after Easter the sun went down behind the houses, and I sat at the top of the steps that led to the street. I waited for my daddy to come home from work.

My mother said, "Go make a fuss over your daddy when he gets here."

She shouldn't have told me what to do all the time, made it pretend. I got up and went to my room and played with my stuffed fur animals. And when he got home I didn't even say hello. She had spoiled the waiting.

1937

My mother and daddy had a fight. I was on the side of the woman I called Torie, who now said she was my mother and that the woman I called Mommie was not, even though I had lived with her for a long time after I was born. When Torie threw a dish towel at me, I switched sides. She was the mean one.

I had my tonsils out. In the hospital the girl in the next room had her leg up in the air with belts and straps. Her toenails were painted all different colors: red, blue, yellow, purple, green, orange, black. I wanted my toes to look like that.

Torie wasn't allowed in the operating room. The nurse said I would go to sleep. The doctor put a rubber cup with ether in it over my mouth and a cloth over my eyes to shut out the great white lights, and told me to breathe as deeply as I could. I saw circles, big circles getting smaller and smaller like the ripples a rock made in a pond but going the other way.

When I woke up, I was in my room with my aunt and Torie. My window was a black square in the night. Daddy came and brought me a beautiful pink umbrella, like Little Black Sambo's, only his was green. Everyone tried to get me to eat ice cream, but it hurt to swallow.

1936

I lay on the sofa with my pants off. I was chapped and Daddy meant to put Vaseline on, but used Vicks instead. It burned. Torie and he thought it was very funny. After a while I laughed too.

Sometimes my grandmother, who I called Mommie but who others called Mutah, came to visit. She smiled and had sad eyes. Christmas morning I woke to find a tree all bright and shiny with lights and icicles. A Star of David was on the very tiptop. I just stared.

"She doesn't even like it," my father said.

Torie had made him get it. I did like it but couldn't find the right words. Torie cried and they argued, sitting on the sofa. It was my fault. I guess I forgot to smile.

1935

A man and a woman came to visit, came to see my mommie and me almost every weekend. The woman I called Torie for Victoria. The man in the brown hat was Daddy. Mommie and I waited hand in hand beside the low stone wall at the turn in the road. Daddy and Torie brought soft bears and lollipops and paid a lot of attention to me. We sat on the porch swing and watched the river flow and the sun slide down behind the house in the middle of the hill. One day Torie and Daddy took me away.

At night, Daddy would lie in bed with me and sing a kind of lullaby. Soon he would be asleep and I would listen to the purring noise in his chest and hold his finger.

1932
I am born.

Nose Ring

LAUREN WAS SMOKING INCESSANTLY, WEARING the soiled leggings, the black dress (one of three—she wouldn't put on anything else), the black boots I got for her, and the long magenta wig her father bought and sent to her over everyone's objections. I'm meeting her boyfriend Leroy in person for the first time, a slightly built man, half Native American and half Irish, he tells me. Leroy, like my daughter, is a schizophrenic.

I was ranting: "You know, you give birth to a little baby and you do everything you can to take care of and protect this baby, keep her warm and dry and well-fed and away from danger. You spend all your days caring for your child and nights walking the floor when she's sick until one day she grows up and turns thirty years old and gets tattoos all over her body and four holes in each ear and one in her belly button and now this!"

"I guess it might be against your religious beliefs, too," Leroy said. He was a student of comparative religion and called me once to discuss some obscure Hebrew word.

"Yes, we're forbidden to mutilate our bodies," I said. I was grateful for his understanding but that wasn't really the problem.

Lauren began to cry and Leroy stood by helplessly. "I don't care what you think, Mother. I wanted it for a long time."

I turned away. I couldn't look at my daughter, my once beautiful daughter with flowing hair, gorgeous dark brown eyes, perfect teeth (hard-won with expensive orthodontia), and lovely nose—now pierced.

I wanted her back—*that* daughter.

Leroy was wearing a black baseball cap and dark sun glasses. It was hard to tell what his face really looked like, but he had nice hands with sensitive-looking fingers.

"Lauren asked me about the nose ring, Mrs. Bloom, and I told her I thought she should do what she wanted but that a lot of people would see it and make judgments. You know," he said, "She's still the same person underneath. We have to look at the person inside."

What Some Friends Will Say to Your Face: One

INT. NEW JERSEY RESTAURANT
Four women in their twenties having lunch.

ARLENE
(talking to Joanne)
You're a real man-pleaser, aren't you?

HELEN
She's a man's woman, that's for sure.

JOANNE
What does that mean?

ARLENE
You know, a woman who knows how to keep a man happy.

BARBARA WALTERS WAS HELEN'S FIRST cousin, incidentally. She was very kind to Helen when she was broke and dying of pancreatic cancer. Offered to take her to any clinic or doctor in the world and paid for full-time nursing until she died.

In the movie of my life, Barbara Walters would interview me at the age I am now and ask all the right questions, such as, "Joanne, how did you evolve and learn to live authentically?"

"Well, Barbara, may I call you Barbara? First, I divorced a man I couldn't hope to please. Then I met Tommy."

The Cucumber Field

WE LIVED IN CALIFORNIA FOR three months every year. Tommy needed to protect his clients from other agents who might be scavenging. We'd rent an apartment in Costa Mesa and from there commute to watch his players for the Los Angeles Dodgers, the Anaheim Angels, and the San Francisco Giants.

Across from our complex was a cucumber field. Every morning during the June Gloom I'd jog around it five times, that is, five miles. I'd watch the migrant workers planting, weeding, harvesting, bent at the waist all day in the hot sun.

Opposite the field, two blocks away was the largest, most luxurious shopping mall in the state. There I witnessed a middle-aged woman buying a pair of Jimmy Choo shoes for $500 and was appalled.

What I'm most ashamed of is that, by the summer's end, I'd run around the cucumber field, smile at the workers, and then head for the mall myself.

Hit Man

$\backsim$

TOMMY, ONCE A THIRD-GRADE TEACHER, was now a baseball agent—which meant he was also an unpaid doctor, mother, father, advisor, and coach. Unpaid, that is, until and if a client successfully climbed the rungs from A-ball to Double-A to Triple-A, and Tommy was then able to negotiate a multi-year contract in the major leagues. Once in the majors the players' expenses would be paid; in the meantime, they lived on $1,500 or less a month, for five months. Spring and summer they trained and played; winters they worked minimum-wage McJobs.

"I had a neighbor stop by the other morning," one of the wives told me. "'I didn't know you had a dog,' she said."

I was learning that my new role, now that Tommy had clients, was spending time with the players' wives.

"'We don't,' I told her. 'That's a big sack of pancake mix. That's what we eat most of time. We can't afford much more.'" Her husband never did make it to the Big Show.

Once in the majors, the boys couldn't spend their money fast enough. But necessities were on our tab.

"What's this bill for $10,000 from Under Armour," I asked Tommy. By then, I was in charge of the books.

"Underwear for the players," Tommy said.

His tighty-whiteys, I knew for fact, were discolored and unraveling, hanging by a thread. "How about a set for yourself?"

"Can't do it."

The baseball business was packed with liars and cheats; Tommy wasn't one of them.

"If there's anything I can do for you just call me," he'd tell his players.

Then one called to say he'd gotten a girl pregnant. He was married to a beautiful, thin blonde and had four children at the time.

"I want you to take my girlfriend to the doctor for an abortion," he said to Tommy, trying to hand over a paper sack. "Once it's over give her this. Ten thousand dollars."

"I'm not doing that."

"You said to call you if there was…"

"I'm not doing that. Ask your brother to do it."

"He did it the last time."

Then another one called asking Tommy to get $50,000 in cash, put it in a shoe box, and mail it to him.

"What for?" Tommy asked.

"You don't want to know."

"I have to know."

"To hire a hit man. To kill my wife. She's divorcing me and wants half of everything I've got."

When it came right down to it, Tommy was just too nice a person for this line of work.

Firstborn: One

MARCH 1987. SCOTTSDALE. FOUR DAYS until the regular season started. Tommy and I were still in Arizona for spring training looking after his players.

"Hi, Tommy? It's me. Guess what! I just got called up to the Show!"

Farfetched plans we'd chased for more than a year through the muggy towns of the south to the soggy cities of the northwest had become reality with one phone call. Tommy talked to his player for a few more minutes, then turned the phone over to me. Gene's wife, Liz, was as excited as a girl being asked to her first prom.

Tommy said a few more congratulatory words to Gene—acting cool, I noticed, as if this momentous event wasn't what it was, the delivery of our firstborn. He hung up with such a grin on his face: "Our first big-league guy! I told you pitchers move up fast."

I threw my arms around his neck, the two of us hugging, dancing around the drab motel room. We'd moved up to the Days Inn from Motel 6—keeping up appearances as best we could. One of the agents drove around in a gold Cadillac and gave his boys Rolex watches. We'd still be riding in the van and eating hamburgers for some time to come.

Back home in Utah we listened to every minute of every game for the Chicago Cubs that Gene pitched. A strike, we cheered. A ball, we worried. But he could pitch every day and not tire; they said he had a rubber arm.

Tommy babied him, encouraged him, buying him baseball shoes and gloves with money we didn't have, talking on the phone with him day after day, visiting him in Arizona, Iowa, Alabama, wherever Gene happened to be.

In the small hotel room where we were staying that winter, Tommy and the club's assistant general manager fought by phone over Gene's contract. The minimum salary had been raised to $60,000; the Cubs were paying another pitcher $73,000. Tommy, incensed over the pay discrepancy, slammed the receiver down. It hit my portable typewriter, taking a huge chunk off.

"Now look what your awful temper has done," I yelled. "You're acting like a baby. What good does it do to throw things? And I think you're being too tough on the guy."

In the end he negotiated Gene a contract for $83,000, still deferring his commission until his player was making a lot more than that level of minimum. That's how Tommy was.

The next season Gene lost his starting position and became a middle reliever. Things went from bad to worse.

"Hi, it's me," Gene said. "I've got a terrible pain in my stomach."

"What did you have to eat yesterday?"

"I dunno. Nothing different. Stuff in the clubhouse just like the other guys, and they ain't sick."

Tommy had his physician-brother phone Gene. "I think he has appendicitis, but I can't tell long distance. He needs to see a doctor."

Gene refused at first, then called back to say he was at the hospital on his way to surgery. It never ceased to amaze me that these boys, who regularly had balls thrown at their heads at a hundred miles per hour, were terrified of hospitals.

He sat on the bench recovering from his operation during the first night-game at Wrigley Field. There was a rain delay; Gene and his buddy ran out on the field and made a game of sliding on the wet tarp. The manager was furious. When Gene was back on the roster later in the season, his pitching deteriorated, as well as his behavior off of the field.

"You better keep your boy in check," the manager told Tommy. "On the last road trip he had his wife in one room and his girlfriend on another floor, spent the night running between the two, and he let all the guys know it. I don't need that. He's nothing but a whore."

"What does that make me?"

"Don't make me say it," the manager said and walked away.

I couldn't figure out at first what made Gene so appealing to the ladies. Eventually I realized that his charm was his silence, the man of few words, the hushed lover in their dreams, a man who slid easily into whatever romantic projection a woman needed.

Management wasn't similarly beguiled. Soon enough Gene was moved back down to the minor leagues.

It would take Tommy three years to sign about twenty players, driving around in the van, meeting families, calling on the phone every other day. He couldn't get number-one picks as clients, so he was hoping a few of his later draft picks, like Gene, would eventually get called up.

The league raised the minimum for all major-league players to $129,000 just after Gene tanked. Tommy still wasn't taking a dime.

That November When We All Lost It: Entry #2

NOVEMBER 6, 1991.

I WAS A LITTLE LATE for the book sale and I didn't care. Chris never did anything for me. When I had asked her to go the fundraiser for a writers' conference, she wouldn't. I left Park City and drove to Heber. The mountains were so beautiful with the snow on them. I kept thinking that Lauren could be dead now and never see the beauty that was around me. I felt so sad inside, in so much pain, so helpless. Just last night I had wrapped two of her Hannukah presents, a key chain she had liked and three bras, a purple one, a polka-dot one, and a pink one that I had bought at Nordstrom when I was in California. How would I feel looking at her presents that she would never get? How would I ever recover from something like this?

I got to Heber in some kind of trance, parked the car, and walked into the middle-school building. Malcolm, Chris's husband, and their two boys were just coming out. I stopped to talk. He told me it was pathetic in there. No one had come. They had some people the night before, but Saturday was a total bust. And then I told him I couldn't talk because I didn't want to be late. I had said I would be there at three o'clock and it was five minutes after. I hurried down the hall past the office toward the cafeteria. I was glad I no longer taught. I got into the room where the book sale was and was appalled by the ugliness of it all. All the books were in boxes on tables, not arranged on the tables themselves. There were signs: religion, fiction, non-fiction, children. Chris was talking to someone else and already packing up to leave. There wasn't a customer in the place. Ten thousand books and no buyers. Chris looked up and saw me and said, "Oh, Joanne, we haven't had any people all day. I was going to call you at two thirty and tell you not to come, but then I was talking to my friend and when I looked up it was too late. I'm sorry."

I was furious. I had a daughter who had tried to commit suicide, and I still came, and Chris couldn't find the time to call me to tell me not to come. I made up my mind never to do another thing for Chris. If you want friends, you have to know how to be a friend. It taught me a lesson in priorities. I thought it was important for me to come there no matter what. I had an obligation. Now to whom was I obligated? I walked around and found a copy of *Marjorie Morningstar* for Lauren. She always liked that movie. Maybe she could read it slowly.

I almost bought some cookbooks for Leslie, but they were still a dollar each, and I was parsimonious. Tommy and I still weren't earning much. Robin came to work late and we talked. Then I took her aside and told her what had happened. She got the keys to the teachers' lounge, and we went in there and had Diet Cokes and talked. She said she didn't expect Lauren to live long. That scared me. She told me I shouldn't feel guilty if she ever did commit suicide. I left and drove home, again looking at the beauty in the mountains around me. I got home around four o'clock.

I finally tried to call Jack at eight o'clock that night. No answer; I didn't leave a message. I did leave one on Richard's machine. *Your sister overdosed.* And then I went completely berserk.

I don't know how it started—maybe with Tommy talking to me about what he wanted for dinner. He ordered ribs at Texas Reds, and

I told him I didn't care what I ate. He wanted me to go with him and run in to get the food while he stayed in the car. I said fine. Then he said he didn't want me to go. I said I would be happy to go. He insisted on going himself. Then before he went out to pick up dinner he asked me to make a salad for him. I couldn't believe I was making a salad. I made it. Then he came back with the ribs and said he changed his mind, he didn't feel like a salad. I think I made some kind of snotty remark like he didn't look like a salad either. He got mad and blew up at me saying, "You're trying to make me into some kind of irrational idiot."

"I'm not trying to make you into anything. I just don't give a damn if you eat salad or don't eat salad. What the fuck do I care? My daughter tried to commit suicide, and I'm supposed to be concerned about whether you eat salad or not? In fact, I don't want dinner. Eat it yourself."

I rushed out of the room into the bedroom. I slammed the door and liked the sound it made. Then I took the flat of my hand and banged and banged on it. All the while, in the back of my mind, spun the memory of getting furious at Lauren when we lived on Point Breeze Place and going into the bathroom and slamming the door. Only it didn't slam with a satisfying bang. So I took my fist and hit the door in utter frustration, and my fist went through the wood, leaving a great hole. This time the wood didn't shatter, and I remember thinking, Huh, the wood didn't break this time. Must be a better door.

I came out of the bedroom and decided I wanted to build a fire, but I didn't want to ask Tommy for anything. All he kept saying was we weren't going down to see her and reward her behavior and drop everything for her the way she wanted. I didn't know what I was doing. I got a Duralog out of the box in the garage and brought it upstairs. It was too big for the small wood-burning stove and needed to be cut in half, but it was frozen. I took it into the kitchen and tried to saw through it with a butcher knife. I couldn't do it. I got a hammer and began to pound the knife into the log. Tommy came in and saw what I was doing and tried to take the knife and hammer away from me. I took the log back over to the fireplace, put it under the apron of the stove and tugged and tugged. Finally it snapped, and I fell forward hitting my head on the stove. I could feel the bump already rising. I told Tommy to just stay away from me. I didn't want his help or his sympathy.

I went down into the garage and got behind the wheel. I wanted to just drive away, and I didn't care where. I didn't want to talk to Tommy or be around him or anyone. I wanted to be alone. I was desperate. He came into the garage and said, "Give me the keys." I refused. We kept yelling at each other, and I told him he's never been there for me when I need him: when my father died, he rolled over and went back to sleep, and I drove myself to the airport; when my mother died, I drove her down to Salt Lake City, and he went to see his doctor about one of his many ailments; when Lauren first got sick, he said he wasn't going to spend New Year's with me feeling sad and miserable because what you did on New Year's Eve is what you did all year. And now that my daughter had tried to kill herself all he could say was he didn't have time to drive me to Provo Monday, Tuesday, Wednesday, Thursday, every day of the week. I told him he didn't have time to do anything for me and he never did. He said he did more for me than anyone in my family had ever done for me, and I told him maybe that was true, but it wasn't enough. Love is not enough. Two people never can do what they need to do for the other. And I didn't want anything from him.

I went into the bedroom and cried and cried, howled like a wounded animal, sobbed and cried and wailed and howled until I couldn't do it anymore. He kept coming in to make me stop, and I kept telling him to get away from me. I was in such pain I couldn't do anything. I decided I was sick of being strong and good and right.

A Prayer for the Dead

TWENTY YEARS AGO, TOMMY AND I traveled to our hometown, Pittsburgh, as we always did, to celebrate Thanksgiving with his mother and dad and extended family. He was forty-four; I was sixty-two. We'd spent the day before with Marvin and Joan, stopping by their apartment around noon. Dinner was at six. There was nothing to help with; everything—the turkey and stuffing, the salad and side dishes—were all ordered from various places to be picked up later. Joan had already had the housekeeper set the table for thirteen.

"We're going to the cemetery to visit Joanne's parents' graves," Tommy told his mother. "We'll be back in an hour."

"You're *not* going to the cemetery," she said.

"What do you mean, we're not going?"

"You heard me. You're not going. Thanksgiving is for the living, not the dead."

"Ma, it's only an hour."

I sank down on the sofa. Hal, our brother-in-law, walked in the room to see what all the shouting was about.

"My parents have been dead for years," Joan said. "*I've* never visited their graves."

"That's because you don't believe in anything."

With that, Joan lunged across the room and slapped Tommy across his face.

Stunned horror. Then Tommy began to laugh. "Is that the best you can do?"

Joan slapped him again, harder, so hard she hurt her hand.

"Ma, we could have been there and back in the time this fight took. And we *are* going."

Joan began to cry.

"That's not going to work, Ma. You can't act like Attila the Hun one minute and a princess the next. Come on, Joanne. We'll pick up the turkey and be here in time for dinner."

The sun shone, but the cold was impenetrable that day. We laid a stone on each of the tombstones—an old Jewish custom—and recited Kaddish, the prayer for the dead.

"Never again," Joan announced at the table after dinner. "I'm never having Thanksgiving again."

"No, Ma," Tommy said. "You can have Thanksgiving, but we're the ones who say, 'Never again.' We're never coming back for this."

And we never did.

A League of Their Own

LAURA SEEMED SHY AND GENTLE compared to the rest, but I saw them all as women who knew what they wanted and how to get it. Her blonde, permed hair was pulled back from her lovely face; her eyes, deep brown, were the color of expensive mink. She'd been living with a pitcher named John for more than a year but couldn't get him to commit. As such she was in the third and next-to-lowest caste among wives and lovers of minor-league baseball players. Above her were fiancées and wives. Below her were those who just slept around.

All of them: dark mascara and eye shadow the hue of bruised peaches; lips, pale; toes manicured. Here in Arizona most women wore loose cotton blouses and full loose skirts. But the three southern girls I sat with chose spandex mini-skirts and crop-tops. It seemed they exaggerated their accents, stretched every word like a piece of soft, warm taffy. All blonde; all with bronzed skin.

At the end of the inning, Dog, the Cub's Triple-A coach, walked up to the fence dividing the players from the fans. He wore his black jacket zipped up to his neck rain or shine, whether forty or a hundred degrees. No one had ever seen him on the field without it. The guys said he slept in the clubhouse on a foldaway cot, he was so in love with the game. He expected the same devotion from his players—and their ladies.

"Hey, Laura," Dog bellowed. "What'd you do to my boy yesterday? He wasn't at batting practice."

"First of all, what makes you so sure he's *your* boy? And second of all, I needed him to help me with a few things." She lifted her petite nose like a miffed coquette. An act.

"You must be the first piece of ass he ever had and now you've got him so pussy-whipped he can't get out of bed in the morning."

"Now, Dog, don't start talking nasty. It was just one little morning practice."

"He better get his butt to practice every morning, or you'll see whose boy he is." Dog stomped down the steps to the dugout.

"You and Dog sure don't hit it off so good," Rachel said.

"Oh, my stars," Liz said. "Will you look at what Mary Jane's doing again. She's determined to catch herself a ball player one way or the other. Some will show off their new boob jobs. Mary Jane, she doesn't wear panties," Liz elaborated. "Probably flashing the pitcher again."

"She's going to pay the bat boy to take him a note asking if he'll be at the What's Your Beef bar. We all hang out there," Laura added for my benefit.

The pitcher blinked hard and shook off the catcher's next sign.

Rachel giggled. "He can't even remember the count."

"If she was back home in Shreveport she wouldn't be flashing," Laura said. "Her mama would kill her."

"We were like her once," Liz said, making a cold assessment.

"We were always ladies," Laura said.

"Mary Jane thinks she's in that movie, what's it called?" said Rachel. *"An Officer and a Gentleman.* Thinks she gonna find someone to get her out of that hick town she comes from."

Liz's babysitter appeared. She'd been tending the six-week-old in the shade under the misting machines, where I wished I was, too. But

Tommy liked me to sit with the women while he worked the stands, seeing scouts and other agents, talking to the wives on the other teams.

"She wants her mommy now," the girl said, depositing Liz's daughter, whose tiny face was red from wailing.

Liz sighed, adjusted her receiving blanket and began to nurse. "Look at my boobs, all swollen up like a cow's."

"Put her on the bottle," Rachel said.

"When I get to Alabama and can turn her over to my mama, you better believe I'm not doing this anymore. I love her, but…"

"Let me hold her a while when she's done," I said. "I'm an old hand."

"When John makes it to the Big Show, I'm going to lie in bed all day in a satin negligée and those little frou-frou slippers and not do a thing but look pretty," Laura said.

"Women don't talk that way anymore, Laura," said Rachel. "They try to act independent and have careers."

"I don't. Neither do you."

"What if he doesn't make it to the Show? And what does he do all winter? Bet he works out and waits for you to come home from your job."

"He drives a UPS truck and his ERA is 1.6 now," Laura said, tossing her head.

"Stop picking on Laura," Liz said. "Your guy's got a 180 batting average. At that rate he won't even stay in Triple-A long."

Rachel wore a hurt expression and changed the subject. "Anyone want a Coke? I'm buying."

"I'd love one, but make it a diet," Laura said. Then to me, "I used to be a real porker… Wait! John's coming in to pitch. He better do better than last time. Strike him out, John!!"

The batter swung through and got wood on the ball sending it screaming over the shortstop's head almost to the scoreboard, but the centerfielder nabbed it.

Laura sighed her relief. "That sure scared me. I can't look, it makes me so nervous."

In the top of the seventh inning Gene came in to pitch. The greens and beiges and sharp white lines of the infield blurred under the fierce sun. Liz grew tense as a batter with a three-and-two count.

"Does he know you came to the game?" asked Rachel.

"I said I would if I could get help with the baby."

And the music kept on playing. Two little boys, four or five, in garishly printed jammy bottoms and big shirts danced up and down the aisle steps, eating red licorice. Players' kids did everything but watch the game. The happy-fan music, the announcer on the loud speaker, the crowd-roar. Three good innings later, it was over. Gene had only given up one hit and a walk.

"He did real good," Laura said, patting Liz's back. "He'll be a pleasure to be with tonight."

"He acts the same, win or lose. Just that dumb little smile on his face. 'Good game, honey,' I say. 'Thanks,' he says. He thinks it's macho not to show emotion."

"Just the way you say you are in bed," Rachel said. She laughed.

"I'm frigid," Liz explained to me. "You knew that."

"No, I didn't," I said. I'd come to expect her shock-value disclosures—and her honesty. We were at the apartment's pool one day. I'd asked her, "What's the worst part about being married to a player?"

"Moving," she'd said. "We're forever packing up and moving, down to Double-A, out to a different farm team, back again. They push us around like chess pieces. We live with a few sticks of rented furniture, none of our own stuff." She rubbed more suntan lotion on her arms and legs. There was a whiff of coconut.

"The second worst thing is killing time while they're on the road. I can't hold down a decent job. Before I met Gene I had a real good one. Flight attendant with Delta. What can I do now? Sometimes the girls work fast-food for a few weeks here and there."

"What do the wives do if they don't have a baby?"

"Shop at Target—since they don't have any money. Sleep late. Go to the games." She took off her sunglasses, turned on the radio, laid back and closed her eyes. "We watch all the soaps when the guys are playing Nintendo. I never miss *All My Children*. We read magazines—I've read almost every Danielle Steel novel. Most don't read books, but I do."

"I bet you weren't frigid before you two were married," Rachel was saying.

"You girls are just terrible," Laura blurted. "What will Joanne think?"

"Tell Gene I took the car." Liz stood, smoothed her skirt. "He can get a ride back. I can't wait around while he takes a shower and ices up his arm and all that stuff."

"She gets so uppity when Gene pitches good, but just stay out of her way if he has a bad game," said Rachel, as if Liz weren't still hovering.

"Will we see you tonight?" Laura leaned back in her seat.

"If my sitter shows."

I watched her carry the baby up the aisle, past old couples dressed in polyester shirts and elasticized waist pants. She was strikingly beautiful.

Nutriment with a Gin Chaser

1981. THE PLANE LANDED TEN minutes ago and still no sign of Mother. All the passengers have walked off the plane. Even the two pilots have come through the gate. And then we see her, framed in the opening of the plane's door, sitting in the wheelchair as if it were a throne. She raises one hand and waves as the men push the hydraulic lift under her feet. It wheezes and clanks, and the stewardess wheels her onto the platform. The machine lowers her inch by inch to the ground. She sits with her back ironing-board straight, pats her hair, and smiles. I almost expect her to clap her hands at me now and say, "Stand up straight." A man in a navy-blue uniform pushes her into the airport.

I bend down to hug her and touch my lips to her soft cheek. "We were worried. We thought you'd missed the flight."

"I've never been so embarrassed. The stewardess asked if I could walk to the gate since I requested assistance. I didn't know what they meant." She lights a More cigarette and inhales down to her toes. "I had no idea they were going to bring that machine."

"I thought something happened to you." I realize I've been holding my breath.

"Nothing's wrong with me." She pats my hand. "I wasn't about to walk all the way to baggage claim." An ash falls onto her shapeless beige sweater that makes her look thin and vulnerable. "How could I back down once I told them I couldn't walk?"

"You couldn't. You had to stick to your story." She looks old, withered. "You remember Tommy."

"I have fourteen bags."

"Hello, Mrs. Azen," Tommy says. "You're looking well." He bows slightly and touches her hand.

She makes sure her ash-blonde wig is in place. "They charged me extra for all except three bags. It cost me a fortune."

"You could have shipped them ahead. I should have been there to help you pack."

"No, no, I managed myself." I can't see her eyes behind the dark glasses.

I push her chair outside to the curb and get the porter to help with the (fourteen) bags. She prefers sitting in front with Tommy and lights another cigarette. He opens his window a crack, drives more carefully than usual. She still believes that Tommy is the renter downstairs. Tonight, the first night, she is going to sleep with me in his place. Tomorrow we'll move her into her own apartment across town.

We drive the thirty miles up Parley's Canyon to Park City, but she hardly notices the mountains.

"I stayed at the airport hotel last night," she says. "I can't believe I made it."

"Was it hard to leave?" I ask.

"Are you kidding? That dreadful apartment? The lamp store? With your father gone, what did I have in Pittsburgh?"

"You'll like it here. I'm glad you've come," I say, forcing a smile. "I bought you a bottle of Beefeaters gin."

"I just want to be with you." She twists awkwardly against her seat belt to reach me in the back and squeezes my hand. Hers is so cold even in August, no longer the thick farm-woman's hand I remember.

"You were always my perfect child."

"I was always your only child. I was never perfect, and I never will be. I've told you that over and over."

"Oh, yes, you are. Isn't she perfect, Tommy?"

"Sure is," he answers. I can see his grin in the rearview mirror.

I stare out the window. It's only the first hour of the first day.

At the house we carry in one overnight case. She walks up the flight of stairs at a pretty good clip. She's thinner than the last time I saw her, maybe 110 pounds. At her heaviest she was 159. She seems shorter, too, even shorter than I am. Maybe she'll go into remission now that she's here.

I make her comfortable in the chair with the ottoman that I had reupholstered before she came.

"Can I fix you a drink?

"Oh, let's see, yes, I believe I will have one. A martini would be nice."

Tommy, intent, sits politely on the couch, being very Old World. She lets him light her cigarette, smiles.

She holds her glass up to the light and says, "This is chipped, dear."

Three drinks later I serve dinner, something easy to chew, boneless chicken breasts, mashed potatoes, applesauce. As soon as we sit down at the table she lights another cigarette, a delaying tactic so she won't have to eat. She pushes her food around and takes mouse-like bites.

"Delicious," she says. "This dinner is absolutely marvelous." She covers her uneaten food with her napkin and lights another cigarette. I clear the table.

"Let me help you," she says.

"No, no, you've had a long trip. You relax." She looks so frail and white.

Back on the chair and ottoman she has a bout of fecal incontinence, soiling the furniture and herself. I shuttle her to the bathroom to wash her off.

She puts on one of her loose, flowered nightgowns with the matching robe, and I put her in the king-sized bed where she and I will sleep the night.

"I know how much you hate poop," Tommy says to me when we're alone. "If she has another accident, I'll clean her up."

In the morning we move her into her apartment. She glances around and makes an O of her mouth.

"I can't believe my daughter would put me in the basement."

Tommy and I exchange looks.

"Mother, it was a matter of walking down eight steps or up sixteen. I thought this would be easier."

"I'll be fine." She walks over to a window and stares out.

"Your windows are all above ground. You're not in the basement," I say.

She wipes her nose with a monogrammed handkerchief. "I had an elevator apartment at home."

"You and Daddy had a one-room studio. You couldn't even go to sleep if he was watching TV."

"Anyone could break in," she says.

"This isn't the inner city," I say.

"I'm afraid to be so close to the ground."

"I'll find out about the apartment up one flight."

"The steps will be too much."

I bite back my exasperation and help her unpack before I go home to make our dinner. When I come to pick her up, she is dead drunk. Somehow she's managed to get hold of a bottle.

Summer vacation ends, and I go back to teaching. For the first time I can't wait. I throw myself into my work, staying after school to jog, correct papers, put up bulletin boards, anything to delay coming home. I pick Mother up each day and take her to our house for dinner. Sometimes we stop at the grocery store, the bank, the pharmacy.

It isn't all bad. Once in a while we go to the Claimjumper Hotel, sit and drink margaritas, and eat one dinner, just the two of us. She likes it better when she doesn't have to share my attention with Tommy. If he talks too long, she interrupts, sighing, saying, "Where do I belong? If I only knew where I belonged."

I want to tell her about Tommy and me, but I can't trust her to keep a secret, and, if it gets out that we're living together, I'll lose my teaching job. She can't understand why he hangs around so much.

She devises little tests to see how far she can push him, then mutters under her breath, "Schmuck." I hold in my anger.

"Tom." She says only his name, turns to the rubbish can, arm extended, index finger pointing.

Tommy laughs and says, "Yes, sir, sergeant. On the double." He salutes and marches in military fashion toward the garbage.

She, who had been so proper and correct, has grown rude and demanding. "Where's my water?"

One night, months later in the dead of winter, the phone rings at four in the morning. I jump. My heart races.

Marie, who lives upstairs from my mother, tells me I'd better come over right away. My mother's outside in the snow in her night-gown and bare feet, trying to get into Marie's car. My mother refuses to come back in.

"She's yelling and acting crazy."

Tommy and I pull on parkas and boots over our nightclothes. The windshield is covered with ice. I claw at it with my bare hands.

"Wait a minute. It won't take any longer to use the scraper," Tommy says. We drive the few blocks to her apartment. There she is, like a wraith floating in a thin, white nylon gown. Her bare feet have dredged tracks in the snow. She hammers on Marie's car window.

"Phil, let me in. Open this door immediately. Why won't you let me in? I'm getting really angry now."

At first I think she's been drinking, but this is different.

"Mother, it's cold. Let's go in." Tommy and I each take an arm and guide her back to the apartment. She looks up at me, her eyes bulging with emotion.

"Your father won't let me in. If I catch a cold, it'll be his fault. He just sits and looks at me with this terrible, angry face."

"Where?"

"In the car. Behind the wheel. What's the matter with you?"

The living room is in total disarray.

"Look at this. I can't find my pills," she says, throwing up her hands, disgusted.

On the kitchen counter, every bottle she has is open and their contents dumped out. Pills, Milk of Magnesia, Kaopectate, and, too, cleaning products: Lysol, Liquid Plumber, Mr. Clean, Lime-A-Way—pools of liquid dripping onto the linoleum.

"Come and lie down. Get under the covers until you're warm," I say. I pull back the quilt on her bed and find the skewer to her rotisserie between the sheets, along with knives and scissors.

"What's this?"

"I needed them."

"For what?"

She doesn't answer.

"Come on, Mother. You're going to sleep at my house tonight. Let me put some warm things on you, and we'll have a nice cup of tea and maybe a hot bath. You're ice cold."

"It's his fault. Can you imagine? Locking the door on me." She struggles into her coat and lets me put wool socks and boots on her red feet. We drive. She's ranting, incoherent. I have no idea if this will last for an hour or for the rest of her life.

I put her in the king-sized bed, cover her with blankets. She doesn't want to get in the tub. She takes a sip of hot tea, but the growth in her throat makes it hard for her to swallow. I lie down beside her and watch her drift to sleep.

I must have dozed off sometime before dawn. When I open my eyes her place next to me is empty. I find her sitting at the dining room table, calmly sipping a cup of coffee.

"Good morning. Did you sleep well?" she says.

"Yes, did you?" She looks perfectly normal.

"Yes, except your father gave me this terrible cold last night. My nose is running, and I'm sneezy. It's all his fault. He wouldn't let me in the car." Her cigarette is about to shed a long ash. "When is he coming upstairs? He's been down there for a long time. Tell him his breakfast is ready."

"Mother, Daddy isn't downstairs."

"He isn't? Did he go out already?"

"He isn't here."

"Where is he? Just like him to leave the house without telling me." She ashes her cigarette. "If he went to the store, I needed a carton of Mores."

"Mother, you're in Park City. You left Pittsburgh a long time ago. Daddy wasn't there either. Don't you remember, he had a heart attack? You took him to the hospital. He passed away almost two years ago."

She doesn't answer, just stares at me.

"But I saw him last night. He was in the car, in the driver's seat, looking at me, really mad. He wouldn't let me in the car. I pounded and pounded on the window."

"That was a dream." I touch her shoulder.

"A dream?"

We sit a while in silence. She goes to the window.

I call the doctor. He discovers he's been prescribing Slow-K while the other doctor is giving her Valium. Together they cause hallucinations.

We talk about death only one time and never hers.

"I can't believe your father's where he is, in the ground, covered with dirt."

She talks about the day he died in the emergency room. "They were beating him up, pounding on him and giving him electric shock, making him jump around like you see on TV."

I don't interrupt her, let her go where she will.

"In 1964 my brother Carl died. My brother Henry died in '72. My mother died in '79, the same year Daddy died."

She's an oral obituary column, spilling dates and details that end in expressions of love.

"I love you," she says, as a small child might.

"I love you, too." My throat tightens.

"Why?"

"Because you're my mother."

"And your friend?"

"And my friend."

The following Christmas she moves into our house. I give her the bedroom upstairs and go down to the den with Tommy. She can't manage the steps. She drinks more and more and eats less and less.

Her lungs are so weak that Tommy has to light her cigarettes for her. Her breath has the sweet, fruity smell of ketosis.

"You can't swallow milk because it burns your throat, but you can swallow gin," I say.

"That's right," she says.

I look at her sitting in the big black chair, sipping her martini and smoking. What can I do? I can't say things that I'll be sorry I didn't say because I don't know what they are. I try to memorize her face, her hands, her voice. When I jog I ask, what am I supposed to be learning?

One night I carry two empty soup mugs into the kitchen and get the meatloaf for dinner. When I return to the table she has gone to the bathroom. Tommy and I sit, glad that for once she isn't blowing smoke in our faces.

We hear a loud clunk and a cry from the other side of the wall. I rush in and find her sprawled on the tile floor, her head inches away from the toilet. Chicken noodle soup is splashed all over.

"Are you all right, Mother? Are you okay?"

"I slipped and fell. Stop yelling."

"You frightened me. What were you doing with your soup in the bathroom? You flushed it down the toilet?"

"You get so upset when I don't eat."

I try to pull her up. "You could have hit your head or broken your hip. What's the matter with you? Why are you sneaking around like this, scaring me? You're impossible, Mother, impossible."

"I had a little accident."

I dry her off and mop soup from the floor, annoyed over the little noodles clinging to the crevices between the tiles. When we're seated in the living room, after I've helped her change into a clean night-gown and robe, she says, "I think I'll go back to Pittsburgh. It'll be cheaper if I go now."

"Cheaper than what?" I ask, disgust so thick in my voice I almost choke on it.

"Cheaper than if you have to ship my body back."

"No, the price is the same."

"Did you check it?"

There is a burn hole in the cushion of the chair.

"I'm sorry," I say.

In the mornings I rush around trying to get ready for school, then go into the sunny bedroom with her tray.

"Do you have my ice water? Where's my juice, my coffee cream, my pills, my napkin?"

"Yes, Mother, it's all there."

"Just a minute." She holds up her index finger. "Let's make sure. My Valium looks different. You never served it to me this way before."

"It's the same as always. Let's go to the bathroom."

"I don't have to go yet."

"I need to leave in five minutes. The nurse won't be here until noon."

"I can't go if I don't have to. Leave. Go to school."

"Mother, we do this every single morning. Please try to go while I'm here to help you. I'll be late."

"All right. I'll go for your sake."

I'm shaking by the time I get in my car.

She grows thinner and thinner, has thirty-five sessions of chemotherapy, swallows nothing but gin and cans of Nutriment. One day she tells me to stop buying the Nutriment.

"It's too expensive. I don't need it anymore."

"It costs ninety-nine cents a can."

"I want to save my money for you."

"That's very kind of you, but I don't need your money. You're talking nonsense."

"I guess the doctor's given up on me."

"What do you mean?"

"He didn't make an appointment for me to come back."

Tommy says, "You have an appointment in two weeks."

"I didn't know. That makes me feel better."

The next day I call the doctor from school.

"Bring her in, although I really don't think there is anything more we can do."

"I understand."

"It's hard for her to travel to the city. I thought it would be easier to discontinue the appointments, but if that's the way she feels, by all means, bring her in," he says. "You know, I never expected her to last this long."

On the morning of March 16th I stand outside the bedroom door with her tray. I hear her moaning softly in her sleep. She has a bedsore on each hip now. I go in and her faded blue eyes open with a start. I help her sit up and remind her that we are going to the doctor's. She gets into her clothes with my help and hobbles into the living room. Her legs collapse; she crumples to the floor. Tommy and I rush to her. It's the first time she is too weak to stand. I know she is very sick. But if I get her to the doctor, he will help. I can't do it anymore. If I just get her to the doctor, he will know what to do.

She can't walk to the car. Tommy and I seat her on a dining room chair and each lift a side. Together we start down the steps. At the landing midway I put my side down.

She only weighs about sixty-five pounds, but then, there is the chair and the stairs to negotiate.

"I can't do this."

"Yes, you can," Tommy says. "You've done harder things than this. Put your shoulders back and take one step at a time. We're almost there."

We slide her into the front seat of the car. I put a pillow behind her head. I'm crying.

"What's the matter?" she says. "Am I too heavy?"

I want her to open her eyes, see the mountains covered with snow, but she dozes most of the time. *Just drive,* I tell myself. Mile after mile.

In the exam room she lies on the table, staring at the stethoscope hanging from a hook. She shifts. Her knee hits the wall.

"Are you comfortable? Do you want me to put your leg down?"

Now she stares at nothing and doesn't answer. I am holding her hand. I see the light leave her eyes.

Every now and then I spot a white cloud against the graying blue of the sky in the shape of an old woman. She is wispy, nothing but air, but she dominates my life. I spend my days saying, "Is this the way, Mother?"

That November When We All Lost It: Entry #3

November 8, 1991. Friday 10:06 a.m.

I'M CONTINUING MY STORY FROM Wednesday. I was in the bedroom crying and crying on the Saturday night after Lauren tried to commit suicide. I didn't want Tommy near me. I didn't know what I wanted. I took a bottle of wine into the bedroom with me and tried to drink myself into oblivion like my mother did, but I didn't drink very much, and it didn't work. I wanted to smoke. I wanted to take pills. I wanted to be unconscious. I didn't know how. Instead I remained awake and alert and in pain.

I told Tommy I was sick of always doing the right thing, the noble thing, trying to be the perfect person. I had to be the best cook, the best skier, the best at everything. When I learned that I might have breast cancer I was so proud of the way I handled it. I was brave and strong and noble. From now on I wasn't going to be anything but a weak baby. I was finally rebelling against my mother who tried to make me her perfect child. I didn't care what anyone thought. I didn't care what Tommy thought. I didn't care. I wasn't even going to floss my teeth. There. My big rebellion.

I finally couldn't cry anymore. I lay in the dark and tried to figure out what to do. I crawled under the covers in the fetal position. I didn't take off my makeup. I smeared mascara all over the pillows. Bad, bad me.

I was in a deep, strange sleep when I heard ringing. I finally realized it was the phone and answered it. It was Rich. I looked at the red numbers on the digital clock and thought it was five in the morning.

"I'm sorry to call so late, but I just got in," I heard him saying.

"No, it's one o'clock, three your time."

I had read the clock wrong, thought it said 5:02 when it said 1:54. I was all mixed up. I told him what had happened.

"You can't feel guilty about this," my son said. "You did all you could."

"That isn't enough. I have to keep her alive. I have to keep her from ever doing this again."

"You're giving yourself too much power. You don't have that kind of power. Even if you lived with her all the time and watched her every moment, you couldn't keep her from killing herself if that's what she wanted."

We hung up, and I laid in the dark. A molar in my lower jaw began to throb. The pain had been bad when I got my period and then it went away. This time it hadn't gone away. When I was at the doctor's the day before because of my mid-month bleeding I had asked him to check whether my gland was swollen on that side. He said, no, it was a dental problem. Now the tooth throbbed in rhythm to the sleep machine we have to play every night to drown out the barking of the neighbor's dogs. I turned the machine off. Outside it was pitch dark without a moon yet.

Every time I swallowed my tooth throbbed just from my cheek touching the side of it. I put my finger in my mouth and felt around.

A tooth was hurting that wasn't even there. It had been extracted years ago and a fake one was on a bridge. Referred pain. I tried not to swallow. I laid on my back with my chin up so saliva wouldn't collect in my mouth. My eyes were used to the dark. Tommy was sleeping on the living room floor because he had hurt his back the Tuesday before. I crept out of the bedroom and saw a hump that was him under the comforter. I went into the bathroom and took two aspirin. It hurt to swallow. I went back to bed.

And I laid there and laid there. I thought about Lauren and all the hard times we had had. The first time she had gotten sick in 1976 and was in the hospital in Pittsburgh, I had laid alone in front of the fireplace on New Year's Eve and cried and cried like I had tonight. It was starting all over. And I was alone again, just as I had been then. I stood by the sliding glass door and saw a sliver of a moon rising over the eastern mountains. I went back to bed and stared at the dark. The night was long.

The phone rang again. It was Jack. I told him what had happened.

"I'm not surprised. Whenever I come to visit she spends at least one of the days crying and telling me how she's in so much pain and would like to end it."

"She's talked about it since she was fifteen," I said. "Maybe that's why I haven't taken it seriously. Eighteen years of talking about suicide makes you think it won't happen."

"I want you to know you're not responsible," he said. "Whatever happens, if she should try it again and succeed, it's not your fault."

"It's not a matter of fault."

"You shouldn't feel guilty. You've been the best mother you could be. I've always been grateful to you for taking care of Lauren. You've done way more than your duty."

Yeah, and you haven't done a thing, I thought. You always get out of everything. What if I send her to Pittsburgh and let you take care of her for the next fifteen years. "I have to do better," I said out loud.

"Listen, young lady, you mustn't feel guilty. I want you to understand that."

Listen, young lady, registered like a fingernail scraping on a chalkboard. How dare he call me that? Who did he think he was? My father? He's not my father, and I'm not a "young lady." I'm fifty-nine years old. He has always treated me like a little girl. All through our marriage.

I can't wait to hang up. No one seems to say the right thing.

The next morning I call the hospital and request a meeting with Lauren's doctor.

"Not today," the snotty nurse says. "You'll have to call on Monday morning and ask for the therapist assigned to her and talk to that person."

"Fine. What time are visiting hours?"

"One to eight on the weekends. Six-thirty to eight on weekdays."

I asked to speak to Lauren. I told her I would be coming down in the afternoon, and she was very relieved. I didn't know what time. I said we would leave at two in the afternoon after Tommy got some work done. He really just wanted to watch the damn football game. I would have driven myself down, but now my tooth hurt so badly that I'd taken the codeine that had been prescribed for my mother.

I called Dr. Low, my dentist, at home and fortunately he was in. I told him about my tooth, but not about Lauren. He ordered Ampicillan for me and told me to take two of the Tylenol with codeine every four hours. Robin called and went to the pharmacy and picked up my pills. She came over and the three of us talked in the living room, but I was getting sicker and sicker. The pain killers were making me nauseous. I got into bed. My eyelids were swollen, thick from crying the night before. Robin was so sweet. She brought in a bowl in case I had to throw up. She stayed and talked to Tommy for a while and offered to drive me to Provo if he was too busy. He felt badly about not wanting to go and said, No, no, he had to see Lauren too, and he would go. Rich or Jack called. I was disgusted that I was always on the phone.

I took a bath but didn't put on any makeup or fix my hair. Let Lauren see how I looked after what she put me through. I was sick of doing the right thing and having people like me.

I knew we wouldn't leave on time.

What Some Friends Will Say to Your Face: Two

I FINALLY TOLD HELEN ABOUT my relationship with Tommy—not a week later, but many months later. First of all, I never thought our affair would last more than three or four months; secondly, I was deeply ashamed of the age difference. In those days, men could be twenty, even thirty years older than the women they were with. *What prowess!* Reverse the ratio and gender and you were talking about a very sick, delusional woman.

HELEN [horrified]
When he's a young man in his early fifties and
you're an old lady of seventy,
what makes you think he'll still be interested?

STEFFIE [laughing]
You're *what?* I was his *scout leader* when he was eight!

By the way, I don't think the contemporary, supposedly complimentary term *cougar* has changed a thing, really.

What did change?: I did. And my idea of what a true friend was.
What never changed?: Tommy's love.

Passover at the Marriott Hotel

OUR FIRST RABBI WAS TECHNICALLY retired. Once a year he traveled from California to conduct services for the High Holy Days in Park City. By then we were leasing space in the Episcopal church; before that, in the Lutheran church, and before that, we met in one another's homes. He looked like Moses—or maybe how you'd think God should look—with a long white beard and kind eyes. He'd been cast as Santa Claus in a movie once, which gives you some idea what Reform Judaism is all about.

I remember telling the rabbi that every New Year's I made the same resolution: not to judge anyone or speak ill of them and would hardly get through half a day. I'd gossip.

"Don't think about it as gossip," he said. "Think of it as exchanging information." What wasn't to love about a man like that?

As our membership grew we were able to hire Rabbi Goldman to come once a month with his beautiful wife. We rented an office on the second floor of the Sage Building in Prospector Square. A bodega opened on the first. Above it, every Shabbat, the congregants spilled out the door. Half were non-Jews, or couples in mixed-faith marriages with beautiful, blonde-haired, blue-eyed children. Gays joined. Everyone was welcome. I liked to remind people, though, that in 1978 when we'd moved to Park City, there was only one Jew in town, Janet Goldstein, a lawyer from New York. Tommy and I were numbers two and three.

My mother had said, "Where's Utah?"

My father had said, "Polygamy!"

My son-in-law, the Episcopalian, had said, "They'll discriminate against you there, you know."

Neither Tommy nor I were very observant, but as time passed, we missed a sense of community—and fortunately over the years our worship community grew up around us.

In 1991 we held our Seder on the first night of Passover in one of Park City's oldest Catholic churches. With no rabbi to officiate, we had no idea what we doing. We brought a Haggadah, the story of Passover, and a dish containing the symbols necessary: a lamb bone; parsley; bitter herbs; and *maror*, a mixture of apples, nuts, and cinnamon; hard-boiled eggs; and salt water. *Everyone's invited!* we said. The Jews were outnumbered by the priest, several nuns, and a few curious Mormons.

A few years later we moved the celebration to the Marriott Hotel. We had a dozen or two actual Jews attending by then. Someone brought the matzah balls, another the *maror*, the hard boiled eggs, the gefilte fish, and so on. All the chef had to do was prepare the entrée and the chicken soup.

The reading of Haggadah began. We poured the first of the four cups of wine. At the appropriate time we asked the wait staff to bring the soup. The chef had dumped the gefilte fish into the soup, thinking that they were the matzah balls. Well, they were both sort of roundish and off-white.

What mattered, in all honestly, was the effort.

In 1999, what had begun as the Park City Jewish Center became Temple Har Shalom, Mountain of Peace, in Hebrew. By then we had a full-time rabbi, Rabbi Joshua Aaronson. A few years later we built an actual temple. I was one of the members asked to carry the Torah from the Sage Building to its new home.

A heavy snowfall blanketed the procession along Park Avenue to our beautiful synagogue on Brookside Court. My friend Carol had asked the police to help us. They cordoned off the right lane of the highway so that we could walk on pavement and not trudge through the three feet of snow now covering the sidewalks. We passed the Torah scroll in its velvet cover among ourselves at three-minute intervals. I had never held one and truly felt close to God. The air was crisp and cold; the only sounds were the crunch of our steady footfalls churning the frozen snow and our singing.

Inside the sanctuary, the floor-to-ceiling stained glass window, an abstract design by a famous Japanese artist, shone in shades of blue and white. Rabbi Josh played his guitar and sang, and we sat in the warmth of our first real home.

Park City is 32.9 miles from Salt Lake City where you can catch an international flight to Jerusalem, the Jewish homeland, 7,028.6 miles away.

Meanwhile, 7,061.5 from there, I had finally found where I belonged.

Firstborn: Two

Don and Charlie's Restaurant was a large, noisy place that served huge slabs of ribs and twenty-ounce steaks, a place with baseball memorabilia on the walls, bats and balls and shirts in big glass frames and photos of players from the past and present. Tommy and I entertained his players there often, knowing they'd feel right at home. Other players and managers and coaches could be found there, too, night after night at the round tables eating ribs and talking baseball. When the minor leaguers were at their apartments, all they ever had was pizza, ordered in. Once in a while they broiled a steak on the grill outside by the complex's tiny pool.

"What's everyone having to drink?" Rachel's half-carat diamond engagement ring sparkled. "I'd like a nice white wine." She studied the wine list while the waitress stood by. "What kind of Chardonnay do you suggest?"

"Shar-doe-nay, don't she talk cute?" Andy said, cracking his knuckles. "She didn't know what it was six months ago."

"Oh, hush up, Andy. I know what I'm doing. And we'd like some pâté to start with."

"What's pâté?" John asked.

"It's goose livers. They force-feed a goose," Rachel said, her eyes widening, "and put a ring around his neck so he can't upchuck. He gets real big and his liver gets fat and then they kill him."

"I ain't eating nobody's liver," said Gene in an exaggerated basso. Everyone laughed.

"Just try a little bit." Liz said. "He's such a redneck."

The talk inevitably turned to baseball while the women nibbled and sipped wine.

"You know, Tommy, you look just like Paul Simon," Laura said. "Did anyone ever tell you that?

"I'm afraid so, lots of people, but I'm prettier, don't you think?

Tommy turned to Andy. "What happened your second time at bat?"

"He jammed me in my kitchen. I couldn't get the bat around."

"You got a good hit later though."

"Is that an Anne Klein purse?" Liz asked. A gold clasp in the shape of a lion gleamed on the front of Laura's white patent-leather bag.

"Are you kidding? This is just a cheap imitation, but wait til we get to the Show. I'll have me a whole Anne Klein outfit."

"What's this? C-O-C—A-U—VIN?" Rachel asked the waitress.

"Give me a steak, well done," Gene said. "I hate to go to a new restaurant. I never know what to order, and if you order something you jus' can't eat, then what do you do?" He looked worried as a kid.

From the restaurant we all drove in separate cars to What's Your Beef. Tommy didn't want to, but I knew we didn't have an option. The next day Gene was starting in front of a couple of scouts, an audition of sorts Tommy had arranged, hoping to get Gene back into the majors.

A full moon rose behind the arms of a giant saguaro, shining so brightly the cactus cast a shadow on the parking lot. The air was soft now after the heat of the day; a breeze tossed the fronds of a palm. I caught the scent of orange blossoms.

Tommy and I offered Liz a ride to the game for Gene's big day, but she decided to stay home and watch it on TV. "I get too nervous."

For the first four innings Gene was great, giving up only two hits and one walk. I took some deep breaths and reached for Tommy's hand as Gene walked to the mound at the bottom of the fifth. He looked major-league in his uniform, tall, handsome, his longish blond hair curling at the nape of his neck from under his cap.

The first three hits, a bunt and two grounders that the infielders bobbled, ended up on base. Then came two weak ground balls, followed by a Texas-league single to let those runs and one more cross the plate. He was down 4 and 0. Tommy stood and paced on the landing behind the seats.

In the sixth, Gene pitched too fine, barely missing the corners. The umpire squeezed the plate so that two more walked. Then Gene grooved one, and the batter smashed it off the centerfield wall, making it 6 to 0. Gene took the long walk to the showers, his face blank as a blind man's, his shoulders hunched.

After the game I waited in our van while Tommy went to talk to Gene—who was suddenly opening the car door, grabbing my arm.

"Hey, you're coming with me and Tommy'll meet us at the apartment later," he said.

"Yeah, you go with Gene and see Liz, and I'll be there soon," Tommy said.

"You'll do better next time, Gene," I said, on the way.

"Yeah, it's only one game. I lost my stuff." He stared ahead, his voice flat and tired.

We parked behind his apartment building under the carport and walked to the front door. It wasn't locked. Gene turned the knob and pushed me ahead of him like a shield.

The apartment was dark. No TV, no sound. Liz was sitting on the sofa. The baby, beside her, woke up, her head swiveling on her wobbly neck, cooing like a dove as Liz tucked her onto her lap. Liz raised her eyes. A sick little smile played on Gene's lips.

"Just what did you do out there?" Liz said.

"The best I could."

"He'll do better next time," I said.

"I couldn't watch. I simply could not watch. You gave up seven runs."

"I didn't give up no homers," Gene said, suddenly a six-foot-three kid holding a bad report card. *But I didn't get any Fs...*

"Well, I declare. I'm not meant to be a baseball player's wife. You made a fool of yourself. How many walks did you give up?"

"About five. I don't remember."

"About five? Well, you better remember. The front office is surely going to. How do you expect to get back up to the big leagues if you pitch like a rookie?" Her mouth tightened into a thin, vicious line. "Wipe that smile off your face. You've got that same stupid smile, exactly like my daddy's when he lost all our money. You won't ever get called up again. They've had it with you."

Gene walked over and reached down to take the baby.

"Don't touch her. The baby hates you too. She watched the game right alongside of me. She saw what her daddy did."

I sat down then beside Liz. "Don't be angry. He feels really upset too."

Gene fell into a chair the way big men do. He leaned forward, staring at his shoes, lacing the long fingers of his hands between his knees.

"I'm not going to be like my mama. When Daddy came home with those big ideas from the construction business and started telling Mama how rich he was going to make us, all she ever said was, 'Yes, of course, darlin', you're going to make lots of money one of these days real soon.' Then she'd kiss him and go on gettin' supper ready. And we never did have any money." Liz stood, seeming to acknowledge my presence for the first time. "I hate my father. You knew that, didn't you?"

"No, I didn't," I said.

"I wish I had a gun or a knife or a razor blade," Liz said.

"I'll get you a razor blade," Gene said. "We got plenty of those." That win-or-lose smile again. "It's only one game. Everyone has a bad game. I'll do better next time."

"I hope there *is* a next time. The way you pitched we'll spend our lives in the minors, with John and Andy and all the rest, in one stinking hot town after another."

"I DID THE BEST I COULD." Gene was angry now. "Now leave me alone, damn it."

"Maybe I should go," I said.

"I'll leave you alone. I'll leave you for good if you keep pitching like that," Liz yelled.

The baby howled.

"Let me take her," I offered.

"Now look what you've done, Gene. Got the baby all upset." Her face was set as stone, and she marched to the bedroom in back with their daughter, slamming the door behind her, her next words barely muffled. "He's just like my daddy, tomorrow and tomorrow and tomorrow."

Then Tommy was knocking on the door. Finally.

Gene did make a comeback. Within the year he went back up and turned out to be the best reliever in the National League with an ERA of 1.46. In the playoffs against the Giants he pitched the only winning game of the four against the Cubs.

The very first income Tommy and I earned came to $5,160. We were ecstatic. We dared not think about how much we owed his brother, Peter, but finally we didn't have to ask for more in order to travel the country, take players out to dinner or to play golf. Think of it this way—we did: there were more than three thousand agents and only 826 players in the major leagues, so, theoretically most of those had only a fraction of a player in the majors. We had one whole client in the Show.

Tommy negotiated a two-year contact for Gene for $350,000 in 1980 and $550,000 for the next year. Gene and Liz bought a big house, bracelets with their names written in diamonds for one another, cars and clothes and a boat—until they had no money left at all. That's when Tommy learned that Liz was Gene's second wife, and he had another child he never saw.

Before the spring of 1992, Tommy negotiated a contract for $1,100,000 plus $350,000 in bonuses for Gene. We were at home the day he signed. Mountain Flora delivered a huge bouquet of flowers with helium balloons that bobbed against the ceiling. It happened to be Tommy's birthday, but he hated any fuss over it.

"Now who sent this expensive thing? I hope it wasn't you," he said, annoyed, grumpy.

"Not me."

On the card: "For your first million-dollar player from your grateful clients, Liz and Gene."

We celebrated that evening at our favorite Park City restaurant, Chez Betty.

That spring Gene showed up for the season arrogant, surly, out of shape, and slow. The team finally agreed to pay another team $272,000 just to get rid of him. Tommy was working with the minor leagues in Florida at the time.

"I'm going home," Gene told him. "If they want me, they know where to find me. And they better give me the money to ship all my stuff home."

Tommy had his first free agent who, in short, unraveled for the next two years. There was an interim contract, an arm injury, surgery. Gene called from his car on a long road trip to say he and Liz were divorcing. For two hundred miles Tommy tried to talk him out of it.

I called Liz at her mother's house to see how she was doing. Not well: staying in bed for days in the dark; not eating, not dressing.

Gene's new girlfriend had told her she was nothing but an "ahm piece." I didn't understand. Liz grew impatient and said, "You know, an ahm piece, an ahm piece, someone that just looks good on your ahm."

In the winter of 1993, Tommy somehow managed to get Gene a job with a team for $375,000 plus $200,000 in bonuses, then he was released—and released again from another team after the first two weeks of spring training. There wasn't even a spot for Gene in Triple-A. Then he pitched for a team for $6,500. During the 1994 baseball strike there was no place to go. Gene was never called up again.

More unraveling: the divorce, the remarriage, another child, a default on his U.S. taxes, then repossession—the house, the cars, the furniture. The third wife and third child left. There was a fourth wife and short-lived jobs in the Far East. He wanted Tommy to help him get back to the U.S., maybe pitching for an independent team.

Tommy tried.

No matter what, Tommy would always try.

Anger (Mis)management

—♭

"DAMN."

Tommy's knuckles were white, his jaw clenched. He planted his forehead on the steering wheel.

I prayed. Silently. *Please let the light turn green.* Every time we came to a red light I tensed. I started focusing on the next traffic signal ahead as if I had some control over its color.

"I ask you, does it make any sense that we've been stopped every sixty-five yards?"

I supposed this was a rhetorical question.

At the next corner an old couple in a vintage Cadillac waited a second too long after the light turned. Tommy pounded the horn. "Come on, wake up! I don't have all day!" I had told him repeatedly that people in California got shot for lesser insults. He didn't care. He believed himself invincible. I turned to Lauren in the back seat and rolled my eyes. She had been visiting us for a week during spring training; we were taking her to the John Wayne International Airport for a plane back to Utah. She lived on her own in an apartment in Provo now.

"Jesus, even when the light's green you can't go. It takes thirty minutes to go two miles."

At last, our destination.

"I'm sorry if I was a burden," Lauren said. "I always feel like I'm a burden."

"You weren't a burden at all," Tommy said. "I thought we had a lot of fun, in the pool, at the ocean, getting your new wig. We had a good time."

"You're just saying that. Look at all the trouble you had driving to the airport because of me."

"No, I always drive like that. And I'm not just saying I had a good time. You know we always like being with you."

"Even the time I came in your room at one o'clock in the morning?"

We'd been sitting up in bed watching a taped baseball game on TV when she'd come pounding on the bedroom door. She'd been hysterical, so angry her face was distorted into a hideous scowl.

"What's the matter?" I'd asked, alarmed.

"You and Tommy hate me. I heard you talking about me, saying what a pain in the ass I am and how you can't wait for me to go home!"

"Lauren, nothing of the sort happened. We weren't even thinking about you. See? We were watching the Padres. Why would we say that about you?" I tried to put my arm around her, but she shrugged it off.

"I heard you. I'm really sorry I came, and I want to go home now, right now." She stamped her foot like a child.

I felt my own temper rising. "You're talking nonsense. And no planes fly at this hour."

"I heard you." She tossed her hair over her shoulder.

Tommy got up and took her hand, looked into her eyes. "Lauren, we love you, and there's no way we'd talk about you like that. I'm afraid you're imagining it." He stroked her hair and made her sit down on the bed next to him. "We never said one word about you. Believe me."

"I don't know what I believe," Lauren said.

"I would never say that. First of all, I would never use that kind of language."

"Yes, you would. You use terrible language all the time," she said, laughing through the tears slicking her face.

"That's because I'm in the baseball business and that's the way you have to talk. Second of all," Tommy had added, "I don't feel that way or you would know it."

"Yes, we could have done without that," I said to Lauren, laughing now as Tommy drove around the parking structure, unable to find a spot.

"I'm so sorry I'm so crazy, Mother."

"Schizophrenia is a thought disorder, just like depression is a mood disorder. Your thinking gets screwed up sometimes, and you can't help that."

"Damn, you can't even park your car here. Nothing you do in this state is easy."

"There's one over there," Lauren suggested. She was always lucky finding a space.

Tommy carried the one tiny sports bag Lauren had brought, and we walked to the gate. The plane was on time.

"I'm hungry."

We'd had dinner, but she'd left most of her food on her plate, patting her flat stomach crudely, saying she was full. Now she wanted a cheeseburger and fries. Tommy patiently brought her the order from McDonald's. She slathered the burger with mayonnaise and mustard and ate it in two bites. I had to look away. It seemed to me I did an awful lot of looking away lately.

When Lauren's flight began boarding we both kissed her goodbye and waited until she was airborne. In that moment I felt nothing but gratitude for Tommy, for his acceptance of Lauren and her struggles. Although a young man when we'd met, he'd never complained, ever, about his role in her life. Although not her biological father, although never having had the experience of raising his own children, he'd been *there* for her, for me, as Jack could never have been.

"You were so wonderful," I said. "So nice to Lauren. Anything you want, you name it and it's yours."

"You mean that?" Tommy gave me a wicked look.

"Anything. I wanted to kill her during that meltdown. You saved us." I put my arms around his neck and kissed him. People might have thought the two of us were saying our goodbyes.

Then.

A few minutes later we were back in the car, headed for the ramp to exit the garage.

"Jesus. There's even a line to get out of here. If you weren't with me, I'd go right over that wall." Tommy pointed to the concrete barrier.

"How would you do that? It's five feet high."

"I'd do it, don't worry. I'd do it."

"You talk such nonsense."

A man in a BMW tried to cut in front of Tommy, who gunned his motor—a warning growl. The guy kept edging his way into line.

Tommy rolled down his window. "Listen, buddy. Forget it!"

"That's what you think!"

"Look, do you see this car? It's a rental. And do you see your car? Expensive. I'm going bash you until yours is nothing but a smashed-up hulk!"

"I want to ask your wife why she's with a little prick like you!"

"To keep faggots like you away from her!"

Oh, dear God.

With that the other driver got out of his car and started towards us. We pressed the switches to close both windows and lock our doors. I sat staring straight ahead. He was a big man, and young, strong-looking too. He waved his fists, yelled obscenities. The line inched forward. When we reached the street, Tommy laughed out loud.

"You may think that was funny, but I don't. I'm through. I'm leaving. I can't stand being with you anymore." I spoke quietly, though seething inside.

"We're at the airport. Why don't you go right now?"

"Okay, I will. Good idea. Let me out."

Tommy sped on. "What about all your stuff? Don't you want it?"

"Send it to me. Stop the car. You had *five* explosions in *three* blocks on the way to the airport. I can't stand being with someone who's so angry all the time."

"I'm not angry at you, just at all the assholes around us."

"When you get mad at them, your anger spreads over everything near you."

Back at our apartment, neither of us spoke in the elevator.

"Come on, shake it off," Tommy said, moving closer.

"Don't touch me."

I had to wait while he unlocked the front door. The security was redundant here; it took three keys to get inside. He followed so closely, he almost bumped into me when I abruptly stopped. "I'm sorry. What can I do to fix this?"

I whirled to face him. "It's too late. You wake up in the morning mad. You go to bed at night mad. In the car you rage."

"Why can't you just tell yourself, 'He's acting like a jerk again,' and let it go at that?"

"I already told you. *Your* anger upsets *me*. I want to live in peace and quiet. I want to live far away from you."

"You really mean it, don't you?"

"You bet I mean it. You say you're going change, but you don't. And I'm glad I never let you talk me into marrying you."

"Tell me what to do and I'll do it." His tone was altered, gentled by surrender.

I studied his face for a long moment. "I saw a program on TV that said some people get addicted to anger like a drug, that they come to need the adrenalin surge. That's you. You're the kind of person that drops dead from a heart attack."

"So how do I control it?"

"Distract yourself. Tell yourself STOP."

"What if that doesn't work?"

"See, you won't even try."

"Okay, I promise I'm going to go a whole week without getting angry, then a second week. I'll do whatever you tell me."

Well, I thought, at least I won't have to go through another divorce. I changed into my swimsuit and went down to the pool. The night was warm; the marine layer obscured the stars and moon. Back and forth I swam, every stroke in every lap, soothing as the tock of a metronome.

Climbing into bed, he turned to me. "I don't want you to leave me, and you're right. I need you so much."

"Enough to change your ways?"

"Enough to try it your way."

So.

For the next few days, Tommy was eerily calm. On the freeway, he let cars change lanes in front of him. He waited serenely for lights to turn green, taking a few deep breaths and humming along to songs on whatever cassette tape was playing. He sat patiently until waitresses brought his dinner.

When a baseball card dealer sent him a bad check, he phoned to explain that the problem constituted a felony and that he'd be forced to involve the police if it weren't replaced within twenty-four hours.

Then.

One night I was awakened by a violent shaking. *Another earthquake?* No, it was Tommy. His entire body was convulsing next to me in bed, rising and dropping back to the mattress like something out of *The Exorcist*. He wasn't having a seizure; he was sound asleep. I waited. On and on it went. Finally I pulled the blanket off the bed along with my pillow and slept on the floor. Next morning, he didn't remember a thing.

Days passed. Same thing until I couldn't stand it another night. I took his hand over breakfast. "I want you to go back to being angry."

"What?"

"Just get it out of your system so I can get some rest."

So.

He did go back to swearing and ranting when feeling provoked, though not as often, and both of us slept a lot better.

Remembering Baby Pearl

Lauren decided to get a job as a dishwasher at one of the better restaurants in Park City. Jack had suggested she be a waitress, that it was an easy job, but he had no idea how difficult it would be for her, taking orders, remembering who got what, being pleasant, totaling the check. She wouldn't be able to handle being a dishwasher either, but we didn't know that yet.

Tommy was pleased over her initiative and so was I. Her hours, from five in the afternoon until one in the morning, suited Lauren fine. She enjoyed sleeping late. I worried but tried to be optimistic.

Each day Lauren kissed me goodbye and took the free local bus up to Main Street. When she finished work, she called home, and Tommy picked her up. Her hands grew raw and red despite the creams I gave her to use. She complained that the waiters were mean to her, told her she was too slow, pushed her around. She did the best she could. But that's not all she did.

Some nights she called to say she would get a ride home. Two, three o'clock in the morning she'd finally get in, hurry to her room, sleep until noon.

The phone rang late on one such night, after two a.m., the shrill sound cutting through our sleep.

"Mother, can Tommy come and get me?" Lauren was crying.

"What's wrong?"

"Nothing. The guys who were giving me a ride kicked me out. I'm at the pay phone at the bottom of Main Street. Can Tommy get me?"

Tommy rolled over, grumbled something.

"He's coming."

It was weeks later in March, the trees were bone-bare. Lauren and I were walking in Thaynes Canyon around the cemetery. She had refused, more than once, to talk to me about that night.

Now she said, "Those boys I told you about? I went to this big old house with them, and I fucked all three of them."

I squeezed my eyes shut, as if that would erase what I'd just heard. "Oh, Lauren."

"I didn't know how to say no. I thought they liked me." She looked off in the distance. "First one guy did it with me, and then one of them said, 'Get the vibrator,' and they used that on me. Then the other two took turns and made me give them blow jobs. I was so scared." She was crying. "I didn't want to do it, but they said they wouldn't take me home unless I did and after that, they just threw my clothes at me and kidded each other about taking me home to meet their mothers and buying me an engagement ring. They laughed and called me a dog and kicked me out in the snow."

The wind blew under a gray sky. I wanted to run away, but there was nowhere to go. "How could they treat you like that?"

"They treated me just like a whore! I'm not a whore, Mother. I'm not a whore, am I?"

I looked at my beautiful twenty-year-old. "No."

"And I've been doing drugs, Mother, lots of drugs, cocaine and Quaaludes. LSD once with a friend. Remember the day I said I didn't feel good and stayed in bed all day? I was afraid to let you see me."

"Lauren, Lauren, your life's out of control. What can we do?" I ran my hand through her hair. "You have to live by our rules, go to work, come home, have curfews, and stop doing drugs and drinking, or we'll have to let the professional people help you in a residential home. You can't go on like this. You've got to change what's happening to you. Yes, your self-esteem is low, but...when you try to bolster it through other people, you'll end up feeling worse than ever."

Lauren hung her head.

"I feel so badly about all of this. What can I do to make you like yourself better? I know you desperately need my approval, but I can't give it. You have to change." I was crying, too, by then.

"I know, Mother. Please don't lecture. I'm doing the best I can. You don't know how hard it is to be me. I wish you understood."

I put my arms around my daughter and tried to hug her, but something inside made me stiffen up. What was wrong with me?

We walked home in silence, past the grave where Baby Pearl was buried. As the story went, a hundred years before, a family had lost their eighteen-month-old daughter in the dead of winter. But mired by snowdrifts, unable to get to a proper cemetery, the desperate parents had wrapped the infant in blankets, dug a shallow grave on a windswept hill at a crossroads, and reconciled themselves to moving her in the spring. Instead the Park City Cemetery established itself around Baby Pearl's grave, generations of miners and their families now surrounding her small red tombstone.

Surely Pearl's mother had felt greater pain than my own. My daughter was alive.

Undertow

My children and I were in Beach Haven for six weeks; their father stayed behind in Pittsburgh. It was already bad: I'd become one of those wives who goes through her husband's wallet looking for evidence—like that expired driver's license belonging to a woman I knew from the country club—I guess she thought it was good picture of herself; one of those wives who hears strange women's voices at the other end of the phone line, like that time at one thirty in the morning: "I love you, Jack, I love you. I love you." Dialing drunk is never a good idea.

"Who was that?" I was furious.

"I have no idea," Jack said. "Wrong number." But the pattern had been well established by then. Soon he'd be confessing his latest adultery, begging for forgiveness, swearing, *Never again.*

One evening at the beach house I put on some stupid Frank Sinatra album and sat alone drinking J&B Scotch on the rocks until it made sense to put on my bathing suit and drown myself in the ocean. I left my robe and glass on the sand and walked into the surf until the water was over my head. I hadn't put stones in my pocket like Virginia Woolf so sinking wasn't an option—I had to swim. And I did, farther and farther away from shore.

But eventually I realized it was their father I wanted to punish, not my children, who might find me washed up on the beach; not my parents, who would lose their only child. That's when I turned around, surprised to see how much ocean I'd have to cross to save myself. I swam and I swam. My arms ached; I couldn't feel my feet. Somehow, I forced myself to take one more stroke, then another, then another. By the time I made it back to shore I didn't have the strength to stand; I just laid on the sand, thinking, *I want to live.*

So, I did understand Lauren's wanting to die, but I was so angry with her that I could have killed her for wanting to kill herself.

That November When We All Lost It: Entry #4

November 8, 1991.

It was three o'clock when we finally left for Provo. I had told Tommy that I did need him to drive me, at least this time, since I was on all this medication and in pain from my tooth.

At the hospital: a replay of all the times Lauren had been committed for psychotic breaks; the same locked doors warning that patients could try to go AWOL. The nurse led us to Lauren in the sitting room. My daughter started to cry when she saw us but quickly made herself stop.

"I really kissed the doctor's ass and got her convinced that I'm okay," she said.

She told me how she understood the system now and had said all the right things to the doctor who had been her doctor in Provo twelve years ago. It was November 1ˢᵗ when she had been there too. I wondered if it was a time of year when she'd always reach a low ebb.

Lauren looked amazingly well. Her skin was broken out, but she had a white headband with flowers on it and was wearing her usual black leotard and black sweatpants. I expected her to look all washed out and sick, but she hadn't looked this good for a long time. She was allowed two cigarettes every two hours. Tommy tried to get them to explain why she couldn't have one cigarette every hour, but they kept saying that was the rule of the hospital. The loss of freedom was good. Lauren realized how nice it was to be able to smoke whenever she wanted, go to bed when she wanted, do whatever she wanted. She said the night before they weren't allowed to have a cigarette from ten p.m. until eight a.m., and she just laid there wide awake all night. If you get out of bed, you get put into seclusion. But I think she liked the strict structure of the hospital and all the rules. It took the responsibility away from her.

We talked and talked. She said she didn't know why she did it. Al had been with her, and he'd taken a cigarette lighter and burned his hand and she'd thought, "I can't deal with all these sick people." She had gone to bed with Tim, and I had told her if she went back to Tim I would disown her so she was afraid to face me. As she was taking the pills she was saying to herself, "Why are you doing this? You shouldn't be doing this." Just the way she had when she was bulimic and throwing up but couldn't stop. Then when she was being taken to the hospital, everything was so dark, and she thought it was the eternal darkness of hell that the Mormons preached. I don't know if they do preach that or not, but that was what she thought, that she would be in darkness forever and ever. She was terrified and wanted to live. She had wanted to know what it would be like to commit suicide for years.

I told her about my suicide attempt then, how I'd discovered it wasn't in me to take my own life. Yes, when she had gotten sick the first time and I'd taken her to St. Francis, I had looked longingly at the graves in the cemetery on the way to visit her in the hospital, but I'd never tried killing myself again after the first time. I told her maybe everyone tries it or thinks about it once.

"Does suicide run in our family?" she asked.

"No, that's just the point. We're all survivors no matter what."

She seemed relieved.

It was easier to be with Lauren than I'd expected. I just followed my instincts and said what I felt, how I had been so angry with her, how scared I had been, how I loved her no matter what and that she should know that I would always be there for her. (The part about disowning her if she went back to Tim—I'd only said that because I thought she really wanted me to.)

Tommy talked and talked to her, told her straight out what he thought, and she seemed to respect his opinion and listened. She didn't have to feel like she was rebelling against him since he really wasn't a part of her family but just a good friend. She wanted him to talk to her tough. He was wonderful even after the hard time I had given him and saying he never helped me. She wanted us to go to her apartment and get some things for her in case she wasn't released the next day. Reed had already fed the cat, she said.

Al, who is blind, is in-inpatient now because he said he gave Lauren the Atavan and feels responsible. I told Marian, her social worker, that wasn't all true. He's upset that she went back to Tim and doesn't want to be his girlfriend. That's really what he couldn't face. Lauren said she tried to like Al but she just couldn't like him as a boyfriend.

Tim came to the hospital to see Lauren, but they wouldn't let him in since he wasn't immediate family. He ranted and raved and carried on. He'd brought her three packs of cigarettes and some clothing. He was very upset. I think in his own strange way he loves her, but he's such a mess.

Lauren said when she got to the hospital they had her drink charcoal. They don't pump your stomach anymore. She said she liked it. Then she threw up all over the carpet on the way to her ward. She was as sick as a dog and swore never to do that again. She said she was lucky she hadn't made herself into a vegetable.

Tommy and I left the hospital and drove to her apartment. We didn't have the key, so I had to knock on Lucille's door and have her open the apartment. I dreaded seeing her. Lauren was afraid she was going to get kicked out of her apartment. So was I. First Lauren set her pillow on fire at three o'clock in the morning. Then she broke her window trying to get in to her apartment since she had forgotten her key. Lucille was nice though. I didn't know if she realized what Lauren had done. She just said, "Tell Lauren I hope she's feeling better."

After she left, Tommy went to the store to get the cat some more food, and I went through Lauren's things looking for the stash of pills she had. I found Dexatrim—the last thing she needs is to get thinner. She weighs about 105 now. I found a bunch of pink and gray pills, too, and flushed them all down the toilet. Her closets and drawers were a mess. I'd need to come back and help her straighten them out. I found her some clean clothes and a bathrobe without a belt and her glasses and shoes. Tommy came back with all kinds of food for her, frozen TV dinners, potato chips, a carton of cigarettes, candy bars, toilet paper. We petted her cat, Boots, and I changed her water, and we went back to the hospital. Lauren was glad to see us again. She was the calmest of all the other patients, but I still had the feeling I had when we would visit her in the other hospitals: despair.

Tim called her on the phone. Right after she talked to Tim, Jack called. When he heard I was at the hospital, he asked to talk to me again. I answered the phone, and he started all over telling me how I shouldn't feel guilty and I had done everything I could and calling me "young lady" again. I finally had to say to him they were annoyed that I was tying up the phone so long.

We left the hospital about seven o'clock. We had been there for a long time it seemed. Tommy had been great. I felt better. He still thought we shouldn't have come down, but I knew we should have. We drove to J.B.'s. He had a burger for dinner. I had two scrambled eggs and toast. I couldn't chew anything hard. I was starving. We drove back up the canyon and home. My tooth throbbed. I was sick to my stomach, and I was glad to get home and to bed. I slept.

All I wanted was to keep my child alive no matter what. Everyone keeps telling me not to feel guilty. I don't. I want Lauren to live.

An Epiphany

WE WERE HOME FROM THE psychiatric hospital. Tommy sat on the edge of bed next to me. I'd been leafing through photo albums: Lauren in high school with her boyfriend Pat; Lauren at camp playing volleyball with other girls, riding horses; Lauren as a baby in her high chair with chocolate birthday cake all over her face.

He stretched out beside me.

"You know," he began, "I sat in the car and tried to say a prayer of thanks that Lauren hadn't died. I couldn't focus. My mind kept wandering away, and I would start over. Finally I finished the prayer and began to think about how I always get so angry. I'd been walking to the car and saw three people leaning against it. It had made me angry. Why? What did I think would happen? I could have just thought, these people are enjoying themselves and having a good talk. And then sitting in the car, I realized I was scared. What if they beat me up and robbed me? I'd been angry because I was scared."

"Maybe I trust people more than you do after all."

"You do. I started to think about how angry I got driving to the Padres game while we were in California last time, swearing at all the other drivers to get out of my way. I was scared about doing the big contracts I had coming up for those two players. So when I'm worried or scared, I turn it into anger."

"Sort of like a little dog."

"Maybe that's why they call me the mad Chihuahua."

"But it only makes your life more difficult."

When he left the room, I turned out the light and lay in the dark. Lauren could be dead, but she wasn't.

No, she was not.

Lady in Arms

WE WERE IN CALIFORNIA AGAIN for the season. It was late and Tommy wasn't home yet. I hadn't had this feeling for a long time: dread. The worry that the man I loved was with another woman. *Soon, he'll walk through that door with the same lame excuses I heard from Jack all those years.*

I paced. I tried his cell phone. I fixed a plate of food for myself. I couldn't eat. Thinking I'd give it to Lady Samantha instead, I carried it to the small porch. She wasn't there. She wasn't anywhere in the apartment. Maybe she had jumped off the deck to hunt birds again. Maybe she was more tom cat than I'd thought...and tom cats had to roam, didn't they? Why now? Just when I'd begun believing what I always said: Tommy came from a tribe of faithful men.

I always knew this would end. Sure it had been years and years with Tommy by now...but, oh well. I'd live alone again. I didn't need anyone. My stomach felt like it was full of cold wax.

I turned on the TV, switched channels, turned it off.

Finally a knock at the door. *Why didn't Tommy just use his damn key?*

And there he was. "She's dead," he said in a strangled voice. Lady was in his arms. She was stiff with rigor mortis.

"I was on my way home. I saw this thing in the street, then saw it was a black-and-white cat. I didn't know whether to stop or not, but something made me pull over to the curb. Then I saw her little red collar with the silver studs…" He kept stroking her fur as if that could, in fact, bring her back to life.

"So, I picked her up and put her on the seat next to me and drove around trying to find a vet that was open. I had to stop at a phone booth and look in the Yellow Pages. When I found a clinic that opened at five, I said I was bringing our cat in. I knew she was dead, but I hoped maybe she wasn't and the vet could do something…"

Tears were sliding down Tommy's cheeks.

Part Three
Safe at Home

The Project of Love

I ONCE TRIED TO TEACH Tommy to float. He trusted me enough to stretch out on the surface of the water while I supported his chest and legs from below. The minute I took my arms away, he sank like a stone.

We kept trying. "Just relax," I said. "You know, you don't have to do every single thing at a hundred percent effort. You can have priorities, like, some things you do at fifty or seventy-five percent."

"Like what?"

"Like cleaning a toilet. You clean the toilet with the kind of intensity a person would use writing a speech for the President of the United States."

"You're kidding."

"I mean it. Like brushing your teeth. I've never seen anyone scrub as hard as you do. It's a wonder your teeth don't fall out in the sink."

"I get it. Like taking the garbage out. I don't have to throw my whole body into it."

"Like putting gas in the car. No need to run to the pump. The tank isn't going anywhere."

"I'll try."

Then again, that's what I've always loved about him: his whole-hearted enthusiasm. Like that time back in Pittsburgh early in our relationship after a big fight. We were at his place. I stormed out, got in my car, and started to drive away. Tommy jumped on the hood and hung on, screaming through the windshield, "You can't leave me!"

Eventually I had to stop and let him off. He left a dent. And, really, how could I give up on a man that determined?

One of the 4%

AT HIS PEAK, TOMMY REPRESENTED 110 players, thirty-nine of which were in the big leagues. But over all the years, John Burkett was my favorite—and his wife Laura, who became my friend early on, and was a devoted, if feisty, complement to her husband. It took seven years before John signed with Tommy—a deal well worth waiting for. We've been friends ever since.

June. Candlestick Park. This would be the year that John won twenty-two games for the Giants. I'd worn a turtleneck sweater and leather jacket, thinking that would be enough insulation in the San Francisco chill. Laura brought a heavy wool blanket, and we huddled together under it. Near the end of the ninth inning another agent stopped to talk to her.

"Well," he said, "our boy got the hook out of John's mouth." He crooked his index finger between his lips, and mimed a trout struggling for its release.

"I'll have you know my husband is not a fish," Laura said. "Just go away and bother somebody else."

"I guess you told him," I said.

But then Laura never ever pulls a punch. And maybe that's what I needed to learn from her: integrity.

She likes to tell the story about the day she and John went to pick out her engagement ring.

"John's cheap, but when I saw what he thought he could afford we got in a big fight. No little dinky ring for me. I stormed out of the store, and he put what he'd saved in a CD until we could pay for the bigger ring. By the time we could afford it, I was big and pregnant and my hands were so swollen I couldn't get the thing on. So I just got a stick of butter and greased up my finger. I'd get that ring on one way or another."

In vitro fertilization finally gave them the twins they had longed for. Tommy and I flew to Arizona the night before labor was going to be induced.

Laura sat on the edge of the hospital bed, her face as beautiful as ever. I wondered how such a tiny girl could carry that much baby.

I remember the end of a game John pitched and won. He came to the railing where we all were sitting. I picked up Max and handed him over to John to take into the clubhouse. Avery, their girl, was incensed.

"You can't go, honey. There are all those naked men in there," Laura said.

The Rabbi Was Right

I WAS BORN FOUR YEARS before the actress Mary Tyler Moore, so what I said to Tommy wasn't completely without context. I had read an article about her second marriage to a physician, Robert Levine, nearly seventeen years younger than she. The two had been shopping for a sports jacket, and the salesgirl asked Robert if his mother liked the one he was trying on. *If those kinds of things are going to bother you,* Mary had said, *then you shouldn't be with a younger man.*

"I thought about that and decided you're worth a few moments of embarrassment every now and then." I squeezed Tommy's hand, and he squeezed back.

"Who cares about what other people think? I care about what you think and my friends and my family and my clients. If someone else doesn't like me, I really could care less."

"And I want the whole world to love me," I admitted. "If the clerk in the grocery store doesn't like me, I'm worried."

"I love you and so does everyone else in the world."

"You know," I said, "I once read about this society in Africa: an older man marries a younger woman. He has the farm, the house, the cattle. They have children, then he dies, and she has the farm, the house, the cattle. Then she marries a younger man and dies. He remarries a young woman and they have children, and the cycle keeps going."

"So someone in the relationship always had something and no one was poor?"

"Exactly. See, in the beginning I had all the wealth. Now you have our property. Pretty soon I'll be gone and you can marry a young…"

"Where are you going?" Tommy grabbed my hand. "You're not going anywhere."

"Not for a while, but I think we should save your sperm in the ice cube tray so you can defrost it later and have a family."

"I can see it now. One of our friends goes to make a cold drink, and we both start yelling, 'Not that tray! Those are Tommy's kids in there!'"

"Something like that."

I wasn't exactly direct in those days. I'd never learned how. Poor Tommy, always having to guess what I meant. He could be a good guesser.

A few months later—the summer of '92—we were back in California for baseball season, sitting in the hot tub after swimming laps in the complex's pool. I began to cry.

Tommy was alarmed. "What's the matter?"

"I'm tired of saying you're my boyfriend. I'm too old to have a boyfriend and *significant other* is as stupid as *roommate* or *partner*. I feel cheap and stupid to be just tagging along with you."

"You want to get married?"

"Yes, I want to get married."

"Why didn't you say something? I've wanted to marry you since the first minute I met you. You know that. We'll get married then!"

I cried harder.

"What's the matter now?"

"How can I be sure you really mean it and I didn't push you into it?"

"Joanne, on bended knee in the hot tub, I ask you. Will you marry me?" He kneeled, feigned drowning, came up laughing.

"I accept," and was laughing, too, when he pulled me underwater to kiss me.

It was the beginning of November before we talked to the rabbi. We'd decided on a small ceremony—very small. No diamonds. No swans carved out of ice. No engraved invitations. Just Tommy and me and Lauren.

"You two would like someone to hit you on the head and wake you up the next morning and you'd be married," the rabbi said.

Now it was December 21. The winter solstice. Tommy was lying on the floor on the heating pad with the phone in hand making business calls. His back was out again.

"This is the happiest day of my life," he said, covering the receiver.

"Because we're getting married today?"

"No, because of Kenny Patterson. I have an offer for him from the Yankees."

I hadn't known my first husband at all; I'd wrapped dreams around a stranger. This time, after eighteen years together, I knew Tommy as well as I could know anyone. There he was, the love of my life.

"Happy the bride the sun shines on," I said. It was one of those spectacular winter days in Park City, the kind photographers capture for travel magazines and their audience of tourist skiers: snow-blanketed mountains; the sky an impossible blue; the evergreens hugging the slopes. Finally we were in the car on the way to the temple in Salt Lake—an hour late. Two *kiddush* cups, check. The *Get,* check. The marriage certificate, the glass to break and the napkin to wrap it in, the two rings, the kosher wine, the camera and film—check, check, check. We'd already turned around once: Tommy had forgotten his wallet. Then, on the road again, Lauren thought she'd forgotten her meds, but found them.

"We have to stop for flowers," Tommy said.

"No, we don't. Let's skip the flowers."

"It'll only take five minutes."

Everything for Tommy only took five minutes. At the florist's I went in with him so he wouldn't spend a hundred dollars. Two freesia, two white carnations, and four cream-colored roses with baby's breath and greens for a bouquet. A peach rose for Lauren and a boutonniere for Tommy.

My friend Robin had arrived at the temple thirty minutes early. She, a Protestant, and the two Jewish witnesses—who had to be unrelated, proving the marriage wasn't coerced—were supposed to be the only attendees. But then our friends found out—Lutherans, Episcopalians, Mormons. ("Do I need a *yarmulka*?" one husband wondered.) There were eleven of us in all.

At noon we entered the little chapel. A six-foot menorah, sculpted into the wall and inset with red glass, imbued the room with a soft carnelian light. The cantor was gifted with an operatic voice, but all I could see were his lips and his crooked bottom teeth framed by his beard, shaping the words to the ancient songs. As custom prescribed, I circled Tommy seven times to show that he was the center of my life—a performance that as a feminist I'd objected to a few months before. But not now. No.

Then Tommy and I were standing with our arms around one another. "I love you because you have always let me be me," I said.

"I never have to try to be some other person. You love and accept me unconditionally and generously show approval and respect. You are my best friend. I will try for the rest of our lives together to help you in everything you do, to love you just as you are, and to accept you completely as a person the way you accept me. I will try to be generous and giving with my time, my patience, my love. Together may we make our way through this world holding each other's hand, doing God's *mitzvot,* and making the world a better place because we were given the gift of life and each other with whom to share it."

"I wanted to marry you the first day I met you," Tommy began. But I could hardly hear the rest. I was crying—and so was everyone else.

What Your In-laws Might Say

⸺ℯ⸺

WHEN TOMMY'S PARENTS FOUND OUT about us, I honestly thought his mother might come after me, show up one day on our doorstep in Park City—with a knife in her hand. Wonders never cease:

JOAN
All my friends were complaining at lunch
about their daughter-in-laws.
So I told them, you know how to get along
with the woman your son marries?
Get one your own age. I mean, we
have so much in common.
We can go get our social security checks cashed together.

MARVIN
She's the best thing that ever happened to Tommy.
She's the right color, the right sex, the
right religion, the right height.
So what's the difference if she's a little older?

Bashert

THE YIDDISH WORD *BASHERT*, OR "meant to be," is nuanced.

An example: I was sixty when I married the love of my life, Tommy, who was only one when I married the first time. But out of the first marriage came my son, four years younger than his stepfather. Tommy and Rich are the best of buddies.

Bashert can mean getting the good from the bad, but it can also mean getting *through* the bad to get to the good.

Woman Seeks Dog

Here's what I think: I got arrogant about my health, and I got my comeuppance. I was seventy-six that year. I'd go back to visit Pittsburgh and see old friends in their early eighties—and, I mean, they seemed *old*. Me, I was still playing golf, skiing, keeping up with my husband, that much younger man who hadn't dumped me after all for a younger woman as some had predicated three decades before.

It was a routine hysterectomy. Since I was still recovering from my shoulder injury—a shattered humerus, three rotator cuff tears, a displaced lumbar, a chipped glenoid—I was out of commission anyway; might as well get that surgery over with.

The follow-up with Dr. Voss, my gynecologist, was scheduled for two weeks after the hysterectomy. Then within a week comes a letter telling me to come in now.

Uh-oh. I didn't want to worry Tommy, so had him drop me off at the doctor's office and leave to run errands. No waiting in the waiting room for an appointment this time; I was ushered right in. *Uh-oh.*

"We routinely send a slice of the uterus to the lab. They found a few cancer cells in the sample. You have lymphoma."

Everything blurred. It was as if the room, Dr. Voss, and Nurse Laurie were talking to me underwater. *Cancer? How? I'm so healthy. Everyone thinks I'm amazing for my age. I exercise. I eat right. It must be a mistake. Sure, my mother died at seventy-two with three kinds of cancer—lung, throat, lymphoma. But she smoked, she was an alcoholic, she'd never been to a gym!*

"Dr. Anna Beck is a wonderful oncologist. When my own mother had cancer, I had her move here from St. Louis to see Dr. Beck."

"How did that work out?"

"She died, but she had the best of care," Dr. Voss said—kindly, I might add, but it sounded to my ear like the punchline of a joke. You know, gallows humor. So I said, "Should I buy a ski pass this year?"

He laughed. "Of course, you should. Follicular cancer is very slow-moving."

Back in the waiting room, the numbness returned. I sat among the young, pregnant women and waited for Tommy. *Should I tell him?*

Then there he was with that jaunty smile on face, walking toward me, delivering the hopeful question: *Thumbs-up?*

I signaled back: *Thumbs-down.*

He took me in his arms and held me close while I cried.

"I have cancer. And I want a dog."

So, I Couldn't
Carry a Tune

THE TEMPLE MY FAMILY BELONGED to in Pittsburgh when I was growing up, Rodef Shalom, was Reform. Not *reformed*, as most non-Jewish people think, assuming perhaps that anything reformed has to be better than what was. Reform meant *out* with some of the old ways. The congregation had been formed in the late 1800s by rich German Jews who wanted to assimilate into American society and not be reminded of the ancient Polish ghettoes from which much of Judaism had emerged.

One casualty at some Reform synagogues was the traditional rite of passage known as, for boys and girls, the Bar or Bat mitzvah, respectively. The ceremony marks a passage for each in becoming accountable for their actions from a religious perspective and responsible participants in various religious services in their families and communities. The problem at Rodef Shalom was that the Bar mitzvahs were becoming extravagant in an unseemly way, as if a competition were being held for staging the most expensive event, and so they were banned.

In 2006, when the rabbi of our congregation in Park City suggested we have a group B'nai mitzvah—which means a rite for both sexes—I was one of fourteen who began nine months of study and preparation. Classes were held once a week, along with private meetings with the rabbi.

"I don't think I'll be able to chant my part," I told Rabbi Josh.

"Sure you can," he said.

He loaned me a CD so I could practice at home, which I was doing when Tommy came down the stairs.

"Why are you singing 'Silent Night?'" he wanted to know.

The next week I again met with Josh. "I just don't think I can do it. Sing."

"Let's hear it," he said. So I obliged him, offering the first verse in Genesis. He got a blank expression on his face. "Okay. You better just say it."

Rituals are by definition complicated, often beautiful and moving, but for participants, nerve-wracking. Having gone through his Bar mitzvah with my son, I knew what the pressure could do to a kid. And I'm sorry to tell you that, at seventy-six, I wasn't in any better shape than he was before the big day. I was still a perfectionist-in-recovery, and I was terrified.

One of the most beautiful and moving parts is having the parchment Torah unrolled before you, standing there on the *bema* before a packed house of congregants, friends, and family. You're handed the *yad,* a long-handled pointer with a little gold hand on the end to help you keep your place. But since you aren't a thirteen-year-old girl, but a woman approaching eighty, the words in Hebrew on that splendidly hand-scribed, holy document suddenly go blurry, and all those useful pronunciation cues over the vowels are missing.

Then, having survived the chanting (or in my case, saying), having made it through your Torah reading, you get to say a few words. If you're prepared with a written speech in English, as I wasn't, this could be the easy part. But sometimes speaking from the heart works.

I had found where I belonged, I said, part now of a family three thousand years old, a family I had longed for all my life.

Loose Association

⁓

AFTER TWENTY YEARS OF DEALING with Lauren's problems on my own, I thought I knew it all, that I didn't need any help. I was wrong on both counts. Epiphanies don't always come gift-wrapped, do they? There I was one day buying bird seed and I overheard a woman talking about mental illness, which is how I found out about NAMI, the National Alliance for Mental Illness. A family support group met once a month near Park City. I signed up for the class NAMI offered, called "Bridges."

For one exercise, a group of us sat at a long table with a teacher at the head as we took a turn role-playing as schizophrenics. "Draw a square on the piece of paper in front of you," said the instructor. The seven other students standing behind us, began reading from index cards: *Don't listen to her. She hates you. She thinks you're dumb. If you draw on the paper you'll die.* On and on went the barrage of voices, negative, angry, drowning out the instructor's voice, overpowering any sense of reality.

It was one thing to know that schizophrenia was a thought disorder, another thing entirely to *experience* what having a thought disorder was like.

One day, standing in the pantry with me, Lauren got a stricken look on her face. "Tommy just said I was a spoiled brat and needed my ass kicked. Mother, why would he say that?"

"Lauren, he didn't. He's not here. He's upstairs working in his office."

"But I *heard* him."

"No. You didn't. Those were your voices."

The difficulty is that sometimes there's a basis for her thoughts. Tommy has been a better father to her than Jack ever could have been—kinder, infinitely more patient—and unlike Jack, not inclined to project his own guilt onto her, as when, after her first break in Pittsburgh, he'd said we should tell people she'd taken a drug overdose. That way, no one would think her mental illness might have come from his genes.

But what Lauren *heard* Tommy (not) say in the pantry that day might have been something she'd *overheard* him say about someone else in some other situation. Maybe those words, his aggravation, insinuated themselves into her consciousness, embedded and festered there. Schizophrenia may be her primary handicap, but loss of self-confidence is a profound secondary handicap. I can't say which makes her suffer more. It's known that some of schizophrenics' thoughts are characterized by loose association: *If I wear the pink blouse it will rain.* In that moment, in our kitchen, what failure in her sense of being cared for, of *deserving* care and love, had triggered that voice to lash out, to punish her?

"Mother," she once said, "please don't be ashamed of me."

That brought me up short; I realized I'd learned from her not to be ashamed—not when her hair was purple, not when she shaved her head, not when she weighed 105 pounds or 230 pounds, not when her connection with reality faltered. I learned to be proud of her for struggling every day, fighting to keep those voices in her head at bay.

"We all feel guilty that we're mentally ill; we feel guilty if we have to go back to the hospital, as if we failed again, and when one of us relapses we're scared to death it will happen to us," she told me.

"But Lauren," I said, "if you broke your leg or came down with pneumonia, you'd be sorry, but you wouldn't feel guilty about it."

"I don't know why it's that way," she said. "But that's the way it is."

In 1967 Alliance House was established in an old remodeled fire station south of Salt Lake City. It was a lovely building where adults with serious mental illness could go every day, including holidays. Lauren's apartment was just down the block from the facility.

Alliance House was affiliated with the "clubhouse plan" being instituted in the U.S. and internationally to provide support, not therapy, not drugs, but education, according to a three-pronged approach: classes for those who hadn't graduated from high school, seeking a GED, a general education diploma, and BBS classes for those who wanted to continue at a college level; a culinary program for those wanting to gain cooking or kitchen skills; and an office-skills program. All patients were called "members"—and honestly it was almost impossible to tell the members from the staff—unless they were members of the band at the facility that called itself The Nervous Wrecks. It was a place to belong, without judgment; a place of community. I volunteered; I served on the board for ten years. At first I didn't quite know *how* to act at Alliance House, but after a few days a familiar sense of acceptance for others as they were, which I'd known from my years of teaching special education children, returned.

"Don't TOUCH me," Stacy had to remind me. She had been abused, but she loved Betsy, who longed to be hugged and carried a stuffed animal with her everywhere.

I became an advocate for the mentally ill. When R.C. Willey, a local furniture store, ran a TV ad depicting a man in a straitjacket, bouncing off padded walls, saying, "You've got to be crazy not to shop at our sale," I objected until the ad was discontinued.

When the state legislature was considering a law mandating a single generic drug for all mental patients in the system, Tommy and I became political activists: *Do you know how hard it is to get patients to take medication, any medication? And now you're effectively mandating that they might get the* wrong *medication for their individual needs?* And where was the wisdom, not to mention compassion, for denying payment for dental care and eyeglasses?: *You want the mentally ill to get a job and be off of the welfare rolls? Then tell me who's going to hire someone with no teeth who can't see?* One congressman we met with wondered if some of the patients were "faking it." I suggested he visit the psychiatric hospital in Provo where our daughter had twice been and just sit there for a day and see how long *he* could fake being mentally ill.

To this day, Tommy and I volunteer at Alliance House on Christmas day to help cook and serve dinner. One member plays carols on the piano; Betsy and her friends eat like there's no tomorrow.

People are afraid of the mentally ill, but Lauren teaches us here as well. She accepts her diagnosis. Someone meeting her for the first time might ask, "What kind of work do you do?"

"Oh, I don't work," she says. "I'm a paranoid schizophrenic."

We also work at our temple. Tommy maintains the landscaping. I served on its board for ten years. Whenever his mother phoned us back then, asking whether I was home, he was known to joke, "She's either with the Jews or the crazies."

I wouldn't want it any other way; neither would Tommy.

The Study of Death

IT STARTED AFTER MY MOTHER died.

One morning, running my five miles on the trail, I found a dead ground squirrel. Each day as I ran by, I'd stop to study it, notice how it became flatter as it desiccated, until it was nothing but a few bones, a wisp of fur.

I began studying every dead thing I came across. Specimens of road kill: a bird or a deer. A fallen tree in the woods that took years to disintegrate.

I learned the Jewish mourner's prayer for the dead.

Eventually I decided I understood death, that I could face it unafraid.

But can anyone, really?

Last Look

∽

JACK HAD COME TO VISIT Lauren in Salt Lake. The three of us sat in the smoking section of the restaurant for her sake.

His face was sunken. I could see the skull beneath his skin. His eyes were dead, pale gray, icy, as if he'd just awakened. The lines around his mouth, his once beautiful mouth, were as deep as craters. There were the scabs of two cold sores on his lips. His hair, what was left of it, was white.

He said he hadn't recognized me at first, as he kissed my cheek. His trench coat was torn at the hem, ripped on the right side.

"Is that good or bad?" I asked, forcing a laugh.

"I'm not going to say either way. Your hair is lighter, more blonde than I remember."

"It comes in a bottle."

The waitress took our order. Lauren asked for French fries.

"That's all?" said Jack.

"That's all I want, Dad. I don't feel good."

"She doesn't eat anything," Jack said.

"Let her eat what she wants."

"Thank you, Mother." Lauren lit another cigarette and stood away at an empty table so the smoke wouldn't bother me.

"She's really tough to be with," Jack said, too loudly. "I don't know if I can take it for three days."

"Why are you talking about me, Dad?" Lauren said.

Our salads came. No one was eating.

"I have cramps," Lauren said. "I got my period."

"Did you take some Midol?" I asked. "Do you have Tampax?" Of course not. Thirty-five years old. She bought earrings and lipsticks instead, in the same dark purple color.

"I'm okay."

"I've lost a lot of weight since Ellen left me," Jack said. He stood abruptly and pulled up his blue sweater. His brown corduroy pants were bunched at the top like a sack, cinched with his belt. "I was 205 pounds and now I'm down to 187." He took a bite of lettuce. "I can't afford new clothes, too poor. I guess I can have them taken in, but I might as well wait until I see how much I lose. My new girlfriend bought me this sweater."

"It looks nice on you," I said.

"Can I borrow some money?" he asked.

The Judaic principle of *tzedakah* invites and encourages spontaneous acts of charity. Here was a broken man I'd once loved whom I'd never see alive again. My act of charity toward him is belated: I wish, in that moment, I had been able to allow Jack the dignity of his humanity.

The Movie of Our Lives: Two

In early November 1993, we went from summer to winter during a one-hour plane ride. Snow covered the mountains of Park City. Instead of saguaros in the sunbaked desert of Arizona where Tommy and I spent April and October during spring training and the fall league, I saw bare-branched aspens shuddering in the wind.

We had just settled in to watch an episode of *Law & Order* when I got a call from Lauren.

"Mother, I wanted to remind you to call Dad tonight. It's important."

What now? Jack always had a multitude of complaints about his life, but he was still the father of our children, so...

"He's so upset," Lauren continued. "I've never heard him so sad."

"Is it his health?"

"No."

"Money, then."

"No. I can't say anymore, Mother, but please."

Tommy was relieved the baseball season was over, the traveling done for a while. Soon negotiations would begin for his players, but for a now we could be home, walk around the trees in the yard, burn logs in the fireplace, see our friends, look out the window at the Uintahs.

This was the first year he would finally see income and be able to pay back a big chunk of what we owed his brother after eight long years of poverty. He would bring in close to $400,000, less expenses— which were enormous. It wasn't the money Tommy cared about; I knew that. Material things were of no interest to him, but winning was.

My movie *Zelda* was just about to start. I asked Tommy to tape it and closed the door to the bedroom.

"Hello," Jack said on the fourth ring.

"Hi, it's me. We just got back from Scottsdale, and I thought I'd give you a call. How are you?"

"Not so good. Ellen left me. I'm really shook up. I can't function. I can't sleep. I can't eat. It's the first time anyone dumped me."

What about me? What about Patty, your second wife?

"And she was seeing another man. We had *agreed* to tell each other if we had sex with someone else. I feel so deceived."

Um. Do you remember accusing me of deceiving you about Tommy— after we were divorced, after all the women you slept with while we were married?

"You said you couldn't stand her, she got on your nerves. Ellen treated you like a king, but it made you nervous." *So what was I missing?*

"You have a pretty good memory." Jack chuckled. "Yeah, we had a lot of fun together. She made me laugh. But I'm so sick of women shitting on me. I told Lauren all about it. She was wonderful, so clear and lucid."

"She can be the most understanding person when you have a problem," I said.

"Yeah, but she told me she didn't want *that* woman around when she came to visit the next time... I live in this run-down apartment.

Selling nursing-home insurance sucks. I'd like to move, but don't have any money."

"How much do you get from social security?"

"About $900 a month, and I make $5,000 a year driving the van for Lowell, and I make about $5,000 a year with the insurance sales, but I can't live on that."

"That's about $20,000 a year, but maybe our friend Jackie is right. There are lots of wealthy, single, older women around. Maybe you should try to find someone who is a nice person instead of a sex object."

"I couldn't do that, marry someone for money."

Really? Morals at this late date?

"Jeanne Shore?"

"Aw, she's too old."

Once upon a time, whenever Jack and I would see a sliver of moon in the sky, he'd call it a "Jeanne Shore Moon," tell me how they'd always considered that phase their own.

"I took her out a couple of months ago to a ball game. Had a good time. But she's *seventy*. I know that isn't too old for a man, sixty-eight, but I don't have money to wine and dine. I don't even care if I never have sex with another woman, but she doesn't turn me on now."

He coughed, a long raspy smoker's cough. "I have to tell you one thing. I know I wasn't a very good boy when I was married to you, but after that I never cheated again, not on Patty and not on Ellen."

Congratulations.

"You could move to Las Vegas, be a croupier like you said a year ago. Warm climate. The cost of living is low. And there are three new casinos. You'd love it, being around the action and everything."

"No. Too scary. At least here I've got my friends."

I checked my watch. "Who?"

"Well, when this happened with Ellen, I told Irv Brady, and he and his girlfriend took me out to dinner. I can still walk down the street and say hello to people I know. I'm too old to start all over."

"You'd make new friends."

"The biggest mistake I made in my sixty-eight years was losing you. You were a good woman, a great woman, and I had everything with you, and I lost you. I should never have let you go. I realize that now, and I'll always love you."

What I thought: *I always wanted to hear those words.*

What I said: "That's the past. You have to go with your life."

He went on as if he hadn't heard. "I told Richard that, and he said that when he was in California with you and Tommy, he really treated you well." His voice was full of pain, emptiness. "I don't like Tommy, but I'm glad he's good to you. You deserve it."

"He *is* good to me."

For a moment, it seemed my own voice was coming from someone else.

Insert Tab into the Metal Buckle

WYATT WAS IN THE THIRD-GRADE class Tommy taught thirty years ago, just before Tommy decided he was born to be a baseball agent—which, as turns out, he was. Now, Wyatt has grown into what he was always meant to be, a healer, an acupuncturist. Tommy says that Wyatt was already a little Buddah at eight years old. I believe him.

I'm the type who's inclined to trust Western medicine, especially since I've been to three acupuncturists in the recent past and, to put it mildly, I haven't been impressed. But now I'm in Wyatt's hands, or under Wyatt's hands, as he deftly, every Thursday, places his needles to address what ails me.

A lot ails me these days: the lymphoma, the vertebrae crushed in that car accident with Lauren way back when, my latest tooth extraction and root canal. But when I say *ails me* what I mean is, I'm eighty-four years old. Paraphrasing the actress Valerie Harper, when she was facing death at seventy-three, I'm still alive, but *long* past my expiration date. I'm grateful. I still ski—nicely groomed runs, no moguls anymore—I still golf—but can't hit 150-yard shots as I used to, so Tommy gently suggests I move my tee shot up a ways—and I still swim in those crashing waves at Lumahai Beach when we vacation on Kauai.

Sometimes when I see Wyatt, I'm quiet. Sometimes I talk. It's my hour, he says. I can do what I want. But this particular day, he says I need to cry more. I tell him that I cry when I watch movies and read books, but that I'd decided when I was a teenager not to cry over *real* life, on cue. Not to cry and make scenes the way my mother did, telling me something was wrong with me because I didn't show emotions the way she did and when she thought it was right to show them. (*Your father is leaving to fight a war in Europe! He could die! So, cry!*)

Soon after Wyatt suggests I learn to cry, I have to go see Dr. McCann, who tells me I have a lymphatic tumor under one of my eyelids and that he's going to have to remove it. At first I sit up straight, trying to be the perfect patient as usual, brave, calm, and accepting. Then I start sobbing, gushing tears, snot running out of my nose, all of that, and I scare the doctor and Tommy half to death.

But, oh, did that cry feel good.

Last year I had a PET and a CT scan, and uh-oh: Dr. Beck found a spot on one my femurs. "If you were a little old lady who sat quietly knitting socks," she said, "I wouldn't do anything, but since you're so active, I think we should do radiation. Without it, your leg might be compromised and break more easily if you fall."

The radiologist and his resident were wonderful. "We're only going to do what we call 'boom-boom' radiation. You come in two days in row and that's it. No complications or side effects." Well, I do have those five little blue-dot tattoos on my leg now that let them line up the boom-boom accurately. I guess that doesn't count as a side effect, though.

I started going to Rabbi Levinsky's Torah study class every Saturday morning from nine to ten a.m. True, I don't like having to be somewhere so early on a weekend day—and neither does Tommy, who came once and has kept on going with me.

"It's okay to be mad at God," the rabbi said. "If really bad things happen, you can go out in an empty field or walk in the woods where you can be by yourself and yell at the top of your voice how angry you are. You'll feel better, and God won't mind. And…if you're having a great day, say that too."

A few days later, alone in our house, I felt really happy. I don't remember why. So I stood in our great-room under the high ceilings and yelled at the top of my lungs. "THANKS, GOD."

I still try to read a portion of the Torah every Saturday: Genesis, Exodus, Leviticus, Numbers, Deuteronomy. They're divided up into sections that take an entire year to cover. My daughter-in-law, Susan, asked me once, "Why read the same books over and over?"

I didn't know the answer, so I asked Rabbi Simon.

"Because you're a different person each year, and you get a different meaning out of what you read every time."

Of course. I'm not the same woman today as I was when I married Jack at nineteen; not the same woman I was, so embarrassed to fall in love with a man eighteen years younger; not the same woman from one day to the next. The mountains around me in Utah grow or shrink every day, so slowly in geological time that I can't perceive their changes. The sea, washing around Kauai, is trying every day to take back the island, even as I sit beside it, writing.

Birth, growth, death—that's the way it is. Fasten your seatbelt. But some crying now and then is perfectly acceptable.

A Course You Can't Retake

As Kierkegaard rightly observed we live our lives forward, but can only understand them backward. I'd be more patient now with my children, more relaxed, less worried about chaos and mess. We'd have more fun.

I was one of those students who always wanted the A. Unfortunately motherhood is a course you can't retake, and you never know what grade you're going to get until the end. And when is the end? When they go to college? Get married? Have babies?

Motherhood never ends.

Out

∽

CLOSETS ARE MY HOBBY. I love cleaning, arranging them, always have. Organizing drawers is a close second. I could never explain these preoccupations until my daughter-in-law gave me a self-help book about adult children of alcoholics. At first I was a little insulted: there's nothing wrong with *me*, right? But as it turns out ACOAs cannot stand chaos. So there you go: clarity.

"Joanne! Joanne! Where are you?" Tommy will call.

"In the closet," I'll call back.

When I turned eighty, Tommy threw me a birthday party. Only my closest friends (see the little anagram in there?: Closets. Closest.) knew how old I was. The invitation left the issue of *how* old open: "10, 20, 30, 40, 50, 60, 70, 80, 90, 100?" Obviously, I looked like an elder—yes, I get Botox for the "elevens" between my eyebrows, and that upsets Tommy who says he loves my wrinkles—but as author Sandra Cisneros has written, we are always every age we ever were. And I certainly knew that my inner ten-through-eighty selves were alive and well. So that wax candle I bought for the cake in the shape of a question mark wasn't just amusing, it was a *symbol* of that every-age-at-once thing.

At the end of the evening, Tommy stood on the landing of the stairs to our loft overlooking our great-room and fifty or so guests. He

241

loved me, he said, he appreciated me, he couldn't have done it without me. Then his gift: a beautiful necklace made of dinosaur bone (good joke, but it *is* exquisite) and a kiss, a real kiss—in public. I might have had too much wine.

"All right, everyone, I'm going to tell you something and then you all have to answer me back in one voice, 'Oh no, it can't be true.' Well, today is my eightieth birthday."

A moment of silence. Then the chorus: "Oh no, it can't be true."

Later Leslie, one of my dearest confidantes, told me she'd overheard a woman say, "She was just kidding, wasn't she?"

Tommy's nephew called the next day to wish me happy birthday. "Well," I told him, "I finally came out of the closet."

"What? You're gay?" he said.

Dear Erma

ERMA BOMBECK, ONCE A POPULAR advice columnist, received a letter from a woman complaining that her husband never talked to her. I was tempted to write in: "My husband never *stops* talking to me. At night when I'm trying to go to sleep, he sometimes stands beside the bed, saying, "I have to tell you one more thing." It takes him a long time to "tear it down," as he puts it. The upside is, I've learned to be a good listener and, after all these years with him, I haven't been bored for a second.

As long as we're on the subject of marital give-and-take, here are a few other things we've worked out:

- He has a temper, but I needed to learn to fight, to not run from confrontation.
- I let him be messy, he lets me be obsessed with organizing closets and drawers.
- He drives like a maniac, but I'm afraid to drive now, especially in the winter.
- I'm frugal. He's generous to a fault with others, but wears his underwear into shreds.

Best of all, dear Erma, I've helped him appreciate life in the "now"; he's helped me put the past in its place. But sometimes, I still don't know how to forget.

What Astonishes

ONE: THIS MORNING, I'M DRINKING coffee on the lanai at the house we rent every April. My seventeen-year-old granddaughter, Alicia, is stretching before her run to Keé Beach. Seven a.m. I can't believe how beautiful she is, smart, and above all, kind. She, Tommy, and I were walking on the beach after a swim in the ocean at Haéna a few days ago.

"In Judaism you don't even have to believe in God. You just have to believe in making the world better," I said. I thought for a minute. "I haven't done anything to make the world better today."

"You made *my* world better today," Alicia said.

Yesterday when we were setting up our chairs in the shade of ironwood trees at the beach, she turned to me and asked, "Where shall I go?" She likes to sit in the sun so she can get "some color." She didn't want to block my view of the ocean.

I am always stunned by what I see when I arrive here, even after visiting Kauai these past eleven years. The turquoise of the south Pacific. The white clouds against the azure sky. The solid green sweep of the jungle on the hillsides. I always say the Jewish prayer of thanks. *Blessed art Thou, King of the Universe, who has kept us in life, sustained us, and permitted us to reach this season of being in Hawai'i again.*

The Hawaiians like to "talk story," that is, to tell the stories of their lives. The handsome boy, Chai, who cuts the tops off the coconuts and sells them with a straw to sip their milk for five dollars at the beach likes to talk story, especially to Alicia. He's lived here all his life in a house down the road where his mother gave birth to him and his siblings. His grandfather was Peter Marshall, the TV game-show host. I'm watching him just now as he climbs the coconut trees, a leather strap, studded with spikes, around his waist.

Two: Last month, I came down with the flu, visiting relatives. Terrific pain in my calf muscles, the backs of my thighs, and lower back. So, off to the doctor: no, not blood clots. Then to the dentist: the implants, the bone grafts were failing. I could barely stand to sit in his chair, I hurt so much. Then to the gynecologist; I've known him twenty-five years. Same thing. I hurt everywhere. Finally I called Dr. Beck at the Huntsman Cancer Institute. "Take some magnesium pills." No help. The drive from Salt Lake City to Park City took forever. All I wanted to do was take my clothes off and lie down in bed. I rocked back and forth in the passenger seat. I stomped my feet. Once home, I tore off my clothes and laid down in the bed. Everything still hurt. I couldn't sit, stand, or lie down.

Then Richard, my son, the physician, called. "You have myositis, a viral infection in your muscles. I see it all the time in kids. Take Aleve and drink plenty of water." In the midst of it all I stood in my closet, thinking, "Who cares about all the stuff you accumulate? All the beautiful clothes and purses and shoes? What good are they? For the second time in my life, I wanted to die. But I didn't.

Three: Lauren's still here! There were two more suicide attempts, two trips to the state hospital, and an overnight stay in a jail cell for vagrancy. But now (now!) she's fifty-six years old and has been married for eight years. She's making friends, volunteering to speak to high school students about mental illness, and asking for help. Lauren doesn't tell them about trying to kill herself, though; she says she doesn't want to give them ideas. She lets the other volunteers talk about their pasts; she talks about the present. And although the voices she hears sometimes do lie to her, Lauren herself *can't* lie. When she learned I had cancer she said, "Don't worry, Mother. I'll be there for you." She also said she'd wait until I was gone before she got the rest of her body tattooed.

How could all this be true? How could I have the beautiful Alicia in my life? How could I be well enough to be here and in Hawai'i again? How could Tommy be so patient with me, considering the four visits to the Huntsman Cancer Institute, one to the dentist, the cardiologist, and the gynecologist, all in a single month? How could he still love me as I turn into an old lady? How could Lauren still be alive, even thriving?

Astonishing, all of it.

Safe at Home

BUCKET LIST:

See an uncircumcised penis. Check. 1997. On a nude beach in France.

Shoot a gun. Check. At the Park City Gun Club. Very scary.

Ride with a groomer on the mountain under a full moon after the ski resort has closed for the day. Pending.

See a black penis. Not to do anything. Just to lie in my deathbed and look. Obviously, still pending.

That's all I have so far.

Sure, like everyone else, I want to die in my sleep, but I probably won't. I can see myself divvying up all of my clothes, actually. My shoes will go to my daughter-in-law, Susan. She's the only one in the family who wears size six and a half. The purses are trickier: the three granddaughters will have to share the four Kate Spade's. What my son and grandson get, I have no idea. That's not my problem. Lauren said all she wants are my yellow hot rollers to remember me by, even though her hair is too short to use them. Oh, and she would like the crewel embroidered bench I stitched years ago.

Here's what I learned from our cat, Lady Samantha: when she was young, she brought mice and birds into the kitchen. Gifts. When she turned seventeen, she came in with grasshoppers, with great pride, a leg or two sticking out of her mouth. If you can't catch mice and birds anymore, well, improvise.

I'd like a little crying when I'm gone, even if Tommy has to pay a dollar or two for everyone who weeps at the funeral.

I don't plan on having pain. There are so many wonderful drugs available. I'd like to be in my own bed, looking out the same window I've been looking out of for the last twenty-two years, next to Tommy, where I finally found myself, at last, safe at home.

ACKNOWLEDGMENTS

To the National Alliance on Mental Illness (NAMI) and Alliance House for their support and advocacy for persons suffering from mental illness, my gratitude.

To my family of faith at Temple Har Shalom, thank you for helping me find where I belong.

To the faculty members of the many Writers at Work conferences I attended over the years, thank you for encouraging my earliest endeavors in writing.

To Anna Beck, M.D. at Huntsman Cancer Institute, for keeping me in good health and giving me the strength to go on, my deepest appreciation.

Many friends have been an integral part of my journey of becoming: Leslie Wood, Robin Frodge, John and Laura Burkett, and Marian Cohen.

My deepest gratitude to Dawn Marano, my editor and dearest friend, whom I grew to love and without whom this book would never have been possible. I owe her everything and cherish the day she came into my life.

Tommy Tanzer, my husband and life companion, encouraged me without fail, and I forgive him for constantly knocking on the door while I was trying to focus on writing to tell me he loved me.

ABOUT THE AUTHOR

JOANNE AZEN BLOOM EARNED BACHELOR and Master of Education degrees at the University of Pittsburgh. From 1968 to 1978, she taught first grade at Greenfield Elementary School in that city, her hometown, while earning a reading-specialist degree, primary and elementary degrees, and a behavioral-disturbance degree. She taught special education in Midway, Utah, from 1979 to 1985.

At eighty-five, she is still married to Tommy Tanzer, now a successful baseball agent, and continues to ski, golf, swim in the waves of Kauai, write, and travel while fighting a slow-moving cancer.

Her short stories and essays have appeared in many literary journals and magazines. This memoir, her first book, took ten years to write. She offers no apologies, therefore, in selecting an author photograph depicting how she looked before she started it.